W9-AEN-486

CULTURES OF THE WORLD
Georgia

Cavendish Square
New York

Published in 2018 by Cavendish Square Publishing, LLC
243 5th Avenue, Suite 136, New York, NY 10016
Copyright © 2018 by Cavendish Square Publishing, LLC

Third Edition

Library of Congress Cataloging-in-Publication Data

Names: Spilling, Michael, author. | Wong, Winnie, author. | Nevins, Debbie, author.
Title: Georgia / Michael Spilling, Winnie Wong, Debbie Nevins.
Description: Third edition. | New York : Cavendish Square Publishing, 2018. | Series: Cultures of the world | Includes bibliographical references and index.
Identifiers: LCCN 2017027626 (print) | LCCN 2017030424 (ebook) | ISBN 9781502632388 (E-book) | ISBN 9781502632371 (library bound)
Subjects: LCSH: Georgia (Republic)--Juvenile literature.
Classification: LCC DK675.6 (ebook) | LCC DK675.6 .S65 2018 (print) | DDC 947.58--dc23
LC record available at https://lccn.loc.gov/2017027626

Writers, Michael Spilling, Winnie Wong; Debbie Nevins, third edition
Editorial Director, third edition: David McNamara
Editor, third edition: Debbie Nevins
Art Director, third edition: Amy Greenan
Designer, third edition: Jessica Nevins
Production Corordinator, third edition: Karol Szymczuk
Cover Picture Researcher: Amy Greenan
Picture Researcher, third edition: Jessica Nevins

PICTURE CREDITS

Cover: MehmetO/Alamy Stock Photo
The photographs in this book are used with the permission of: 1 Vahan Abrahamyan/Shutterstock.com; p. 3 Grisha Bruev/Shutterstock.com; p. 5 My Good Images/Shutterstock.com; p. 6 Grisha Bruev/Shutterstock.com; p. 8 Stringer/Anadolu Agency/Getty Images; p. 9 VANO SHLAMOV/AFP/ Getty Images; p. 10 Harvepino/Shutterstock.com; p. 11 Rainer Lesniewski/Shutterstock.com; p. 13 Andrew Mayovskyy/Shutterstock.com; p. 14 Aleksandar Todorovic/Shutterstock.com; p. 15 alfotokunst/Shutterstock.com; p. 16 posztos/Shutterstock.com; p. 17 LALS STOCK/Shutterstock.com; p. 18 SARYMSAKOV ANDREY/Shutterstock.com; p. 20 Ulrich Prokop/Wikimedia Commons/ File:Common Pheasant (Hybride).jpg; p. 21 Alexandr Junek Imaging/Shutterstock.com; p. 22 Vitaly Titov/Shutterstock.com; p. 24 Colchians /Wikimedia Commons/ File:MÖ 6. yüzyıla ait gümüş Kolkhis sikkesi.jpg/CC-PD-Mark; p. 25 Deu, basiert auf Andrew Anderson's File:Earlycaucasus655.jpg und Don-Kun's File:Caucasus 300 map alt de.png/ Wikimedia Commons/ File:Georgian States Colchis and Iberia (600-150BC)-en.svg; p. 26 Konstantinos Volanakis/Wikimedia Commons/ File:Constantine Volanakis Argo.jpg; p. 28 Curioso/Shutterstock.com; p. 31 Unknown /Wikimedia Commons/File:Treaty of Georgievsk of 1783 (Esadze, 1913).JPG; p. 32 sebos/Shutterstock.com; p. 34 VANO SHLAMOV/AFP/Getty Images; p. 36 Ssolbergj & creator of source map /Wikimedia Commons/File:Georgia, Ossetia, Russia and Abkhazia (en).svg/CC-BY-SA-3.0; p. 38 Yulia Grigoryeva/Shutterstock.com; p. 40 Oleh Dubyna/Shutterstock.com; p. 41 Gabriel Petrescu/Shutterstock.com; p. 42 Mamuka Gotsiridze/Shutterstock.com; p. 43 AP Photo/ Shakh Aivazov; p. 44 Kharkhan Oleg/Shutterstock.com; p. 46 Artstyle Studio/Shutterstock.com; p. 48 VANO SHLAMOV/AFP/Getty Images; p. 50 VANO SHLAMOV/AFP/Getty Images; p. 53 Andrii Lutsyk/ Shutterstock.com; p. 54 Andrew Mayovskyy/Shutterstock.com; p. 55 Alex Shlamov/Anadolu Agency/Getty Images; p. 56 eFesenko/Shutterstock.com; p. 57 Biskariot/Shutterstock.com; p. 58 Jean-Philippe Tournut/Moment Unreleased/Getty Images; p. 60 koss13/Shutterstock.com; p. 61 MehmetO/ Shutterstock.com; p. 62 Grisha Bruev/Shutterstock.com; p. 65 Ivan Vdovin/AWL Images/Getty Images; p. 66 VIKTOR DRACHEV/AFP/Getty Images; p. 68 MehmetO/Shutterstock.com; p. 70 eFesenko/Shutterstock.com; p. 71 Lerner Vadim/Shutterstock.com; p. 73 Elena Rostunova/Shutterstock.com; p. 76 VANO SHLAMOV/AFP/GettyImages; p. 78 Andrei Bortnikau/Shutterstock.com; p. 80 Vladimir Zhoga/Shutterstock.com; p. 82 Bill Perry/Shutterstock. com; p. 84 Vladimir Zhoga/Shutterstock.com; p. 86 Igor_Astakhovi/Shutterstock.com; p. 88 Artem Mishukov/Shutterstock.com.; p. 89 Radiokafka/ Shutterstock.com; p. 90 ET1972/Shutterstock.com; p. 94 Grisha Bruev/Shutterstock.com; p. 96 Radiokafka/Shutterstock.com; p. 97 Graeb, Carl Georg Anton/Wikimedia Commons/ File:(BL) GEORGIAN NOBLEMAN'S HOUSE IN TIFLIS.jpg; p. 98 MehmetO/Shutterstock.com; p. 99 Milosz Maslanka/ Shutterstock.com; p. 103 Fine Art Images/Heritage Images/Getty Images; p. 104 MehmetO/Shutterstock.com ; p. 106 Dontsov Evgeny/Shutterstock. com; p. 108 thomas koch/Shutterstock.com; p. 109 Dmytro Vietrov/Shutterstock.com; p. 110 Radiokafka/Shutterstock.com; p. 112 Alena Kuzmina/ Shutterstock.com; p. 114 Grisha Bruev/Shutterstock.com; p. 116 posztos/Shutterstock.com; p. 117 MIKHEIL/Wikimedia Commons/ File:Chichilaki 8.jpg/ CC BY-SA 4.0; p. 118 Igor_Astakhovi/Shutterstock.com; p. 120 Radiokafka/Shutterstock.com; p. 122 Grisha Bruev/Shutterstock.com; p. 123 Andrii Zhezhera/Shutterstock.com; p. 124 anfoto/Shutterstock.com; p. 125 Elena Mirage/Shutterstock.com; p. 126 Radiokafka/Shutterstock.com; p. 127 Elena Hramova/Shutterstock.com; p. 128 Yulia Grigoryeva/Shutterstock.com; p. 129 Radiokafka/Shutterstock.com; p. 130 zloitapok/Shutterstock. com; p. 131 Rui Elena/Shutterstock.com; p. 137 Vectorov/Shutterstock.com.

PRECEDING PAGE

A statue of Medea holding the Golden Fleece stands in Batumi, Georgia.

Printed in the United States of America

CONTENTS

GEORGIA TODAY

GEORGIA IS A COUNTRY THAT HAPPENS TO HAVE THE SAME NAME as one of the US states. The two have no connection. Georgia the country is located in the Caucasus region on the eastern side of the Black Sea. That huge body of water lies between Eastern Europe and Western Asia, and flows, by way of various straits and the smaller Sea of Marmara, to the Aegean Sea and on to the Mediterranean.

The Caucasus is the land that lies between the Black Sea and the Caspian Sea. The Caucasus Mountains themselves—the Greater and Lesser ranges—which run along the northern and southern borders of Georgia, have helped shape the country's vibrant history and culture. Higher than the Alps, the mountains give Georgia unsurpassed vistas of natural beauty. Creating a geographical barrier, the peaks have protected ancient mountain cultures, languages, and architecture. Much of this beautiful land was off-limits to the West during the past century, closed off by the Iron Curtain. That's the metaphorical name for the boundary between the communist nations of Soviet-dominated Eastern Europe and the democratic nations of the West.

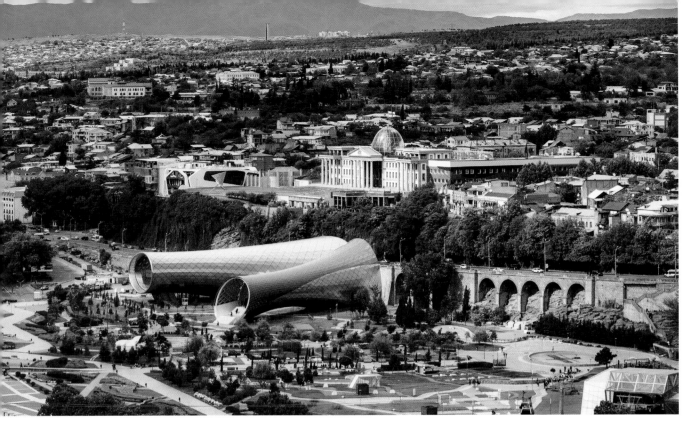

The eccentric glass-and-steel Tbilisi Music Theater and Exhibition Hall in Rike Park, which opened in 2016, is meant to be a "periscope to the city."

Today, however, modern Georgia is trying to capitalize on its amazing natural and cultural assets by promoting its tourism industry. A major key to success in that endeavor will depend on Georgia's ability to maintain peace, security, and stability. So far, it has been doing fairly well, but there are problems.

Georgia borders on Russia to the north, and like many of Russia's immediate neighbors, it was once a republic of the Soviet Union, which existed from 1922 to 1991. The Union of Soviet Socialist Republics (USSR) was—as its name states—a coalition of socialist countries with a centralized economy and a centralized government ruled by one party—the Communist Party. The capital was Moscow. In theory, the fifteen constituent republics shared power equally, but in reality Russia was by far the dominant force. Many of the Soviet republics were unwilling participants in the union to begin with. Georgia was one of them.

When the Soviet Union fell apart in 1991, Georgia became an independent country once again. Since that time, it has been trying to create itself as a representative, democratic republic with a multi-party system. But it's been tough going. For one thing, Georgia has had little experience as an independent country, with much of its history spent under the domination of other empires, including the Russian Empire in the nineteen century. And after two centuries of Russian domination, Georgia is finding it to be difficult—at times, impossible—to be free of its powerful, looming neighbor.

Since independence, two regions within Georgia, Abkhazia and South Ossetia, have broken away from the nation and declared their own independence. Both are supported by Russia, which may be trying to absorb them, just as it did Ukraine's Crimean Peninsula in 2014. Georgia's borders with both areas—which still officially belong to Georgia—are patrolled by Russian troops. In 2008, tensions between Georgia and Russia over the status of South Ossetia broke out in hostilities—a short but deadly war. Georgia believes the Russians are there for more than just show. However, Russia says its soldiers are there to protect the South Ossetians from Georgian aggression, so the complicated issue hinges on a matter of perspective.

In 2017, a poll of the Georgian people revealed that a majority of them—63 percent—considered Russia to be the greatest threat to their country. The poll, conducted by the National Democratic Institute (NDI) and the Caucasus Research Resource Center (CRRC Georgia), also found more than 40 percent of Georgians said Russia had a negative impact on the country's economy, security, and politics.

Just as the Black Sea waters flow away from Russia and toward Europe, Georgian sentiment seems to be following the same course. Situated literally on the border between Asia and Europe, this Eurasian country is looking to Europe to find a model for its future. Some 80 percent of Georgians support joining the European Union (EU), an economic alliance of European nations. But others fear doing so would anger and provoke the Russian bear.

Fear of Russia could also be driving Georgian support for joining NATO. The North Atlantic Treaty Organization (NATO) is a mutual defense alliance between North American and European nations that was established after World War II specifically for protection against Russian aggression. Georgia is not a member of either organization as yet, but in February 2017 it concluded

A Georgian woman holds the flags of the European Union and Georgia to celebrate new visa-free travel throughout the Schengen Area in 2017.

a visa liberalization agreement with the EU. This grants Georgians visa-free travel privileges to the Schengen Area, a coalition of open-border nations made up of most EU and some non-EU members. This is a clear sign that relations between Europe and Georgia are warming.

Ironically though, in light of these findings, Georgians are nearly divided on whether the dissolution of the Soviet Union was a good (48 percent) or bad development (42 percent) for the country. Some people, particularly older folks and minority groups, look back at the Soviet era as being more stable, and find the current situation to be less certain.

One certainty in Georgia is the Georgian Orthodox Church. Although the predominately Christian nation's constitution protects religious freedom, the Church wields a mighty influence over its society, culture, economics, and politics. Headed by the aging Catholicos-Patriarch, Ilia II, the Church provides a stabilizing force as Georgians face the rapid-fire developments of today's world. However, in some ways, traditional Orthodox values bump against European and Western values, causing friction where the two cultures collide. In particular, the Georgian Orthodox Church takes a very conservative view of social and family matters. These include its stances in matters of universal human rights—women's issues, domestic violence, sexual and gender orientation, and same-sex marriage. The Church is also actively, and legally, involved in the government's finances and politics, leaving no pretense of separation of church and state.

As Georgia continues to develop itself as an independent nation in the twenty-first century, it will need to face these challenges, and many others. Much will depend on Russian leader Vladimir Putin's plans for the region—which remain unclear even as he boldly annexes his neighbor's territories and nibbles away at Georgia's borders. Much will also depend on how far Georgia leans toward the West, and whether it can meet the qualifying demands of EU and NATO membership. And finally, much will depend on the Georgian people themselves and their government's ability to clean its own house of corruption and other endemic problems. Stuck between Asia and Europe, the East and the West, the Church and the state, Georgia has quite a balancing act to perform!

Georgians rally in front of the parliament building in Tbilisi to show their support for women's rights on International Women's Day 2017.

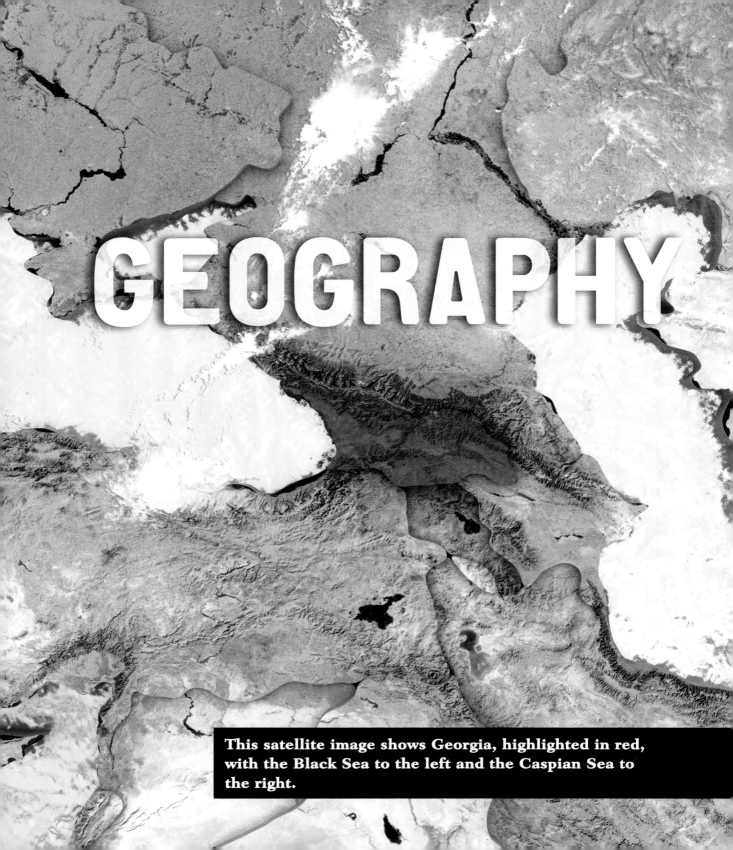

GEOGRAPHY

This satellite image shows Georgia, highlighted in red, with the Black Sea to the left and the Caspian Sea to the right.

GEORGIA IS A RELATIVELY SMALL country straddling two continents, Europe and Asia. Given that the line between Europe and Asia is an imaginary, human-made division and not a natural one, the exact border is subject to disagreement. The region in general, therefore, is sometimes referred to as Eurasia.

1

What lands constitute today's Georgia is a matter of political, rather than geographic, determination, and the political boundaries have been in flux for years. Most maps, including some of the ones in this book, will show Georgia incorporating the provinces of Abkhazia, South Ossetia, and Ajaria. However the people who live in those parts may have a very different view.

This map includes the breakaway regions of Abkhazia and South Ossetia, as well as the autonomous region of Ajaria (Adjara).

However, Eurasia is also the name for the huge landmass that contains the two continents, so the term can be confusing. According to the *CIA World Factbook*, the easternmost border of Europe runs along the Ural Mountains and the Ural River; on the southeast, it follows the Caspian Sea; and on the south, the Caucasus Mountains, the Black Sea, and the Mediterranean. Therefore, portions of Azerbaijan, Georgia, Kazakhstan, Russia, and Turkey fall within both Europe and Asia.

However, many sources, including the United Nations classification of world regions, National Geographic, and the *Encyclopaedia Britannica*, place Georgia in Asia. Others, such as *Merriam-Webster's Collegiate Dictionary*, the BBC, and others, put it in Europe. The CIA World Factbook locates the country mostly in Southwestern Asia, with "a sliver of land north of Caucasus extending into Europe" and notes that "Georgia views itself as part of Europe; geopolitically, it can be classified as falling within Europe, the Middle East, or both."

Situated in the heart of the Caucasus mountain range, on the eastern coast of the Black Sea, Georgia is separated from its giant northern neighbor, Russia, by 450 miles (723 kilometers) of mountains. To the east lies Azerbaijan, to the south Turkey, and to the southeast, Armenia. Surrounded by mountains and sea, the country is geographically self-contained, and this has helped it preserve its identity and culture despite many foreign invasions.

Georgia covers an area of about 26,900 square miles (69,700 sq km)—slightly smaller than South Carolina and slightly larger than West Virginia. (However, this size estimation includes the breakaways provinces of Abkhazia and South Ossetia, which, as of 2017, are *de facto* administrative regions of Russia. Georgia considers these provinces "occupied territories.")

Although 87 percent of Georgia is largely mountainous, the small nation has a remarkably varied climate, ranging from warm subtropics on the Black Sea coast to cold winters in the ice-capped peaks of the Caucasus.

FROM MOUNTAIN PEAKS TO SWAMPY LOWLAND

Georgia can be roughly divided into three main geographical areas: the Great Caucasus range, the central lowlands, and the Lesser Caucasus.

THE GREAT CAUCASUS Higher than the Swiss Alps, the Great Caucasus range dominates the landscape of northern Georgia. The mountain belts rise from the east and are often separated by deep gorges. The Bokovoy range is northernmost; farther south the most important spurs are those of the Lomisi and Kartli ranges. The cone of Mount Kazbek, an extinct volcano, dominates the Bokovoy range at a height of 16,558 feet (5,047 meters). Georgia's spectacular crest-lined peaks also include Mount Shkhara (16,627 feet/5,066 m), Mount Tetnuldi (15,938 feet/ 4,858 m), and Mount Ushba (15,419 feet/4,700 m)—all in the region of Upper Svaneti—and Mount Rustaveli (15,944 feet/4,860 m) to the southeast.

The wooded gorges and valleys in bloom have been a great lure for writers and travelers throughout the ages, including Russian writers Alexander Pushkin, Mikhail Lermontov, Lev Nikolaevich Tolstoy, and Maxim Gorky, as well as French writer Alexandre Dumas. Lermontov, for example, described the Krestovy Pass in his novel *A Hero of Our Time* (1840), writing, "What a delightful place, that valley! On all sides rise inaccessible mountains, reddish cliffs hung over with great ivy crowned with clumps of plane trees; tawny precipices streaked with washes, and far above the golden fringe of

Colorful autumn leaves frame Mount Ushba in the Caucasus Mountains.

The Svaneti Region is the highest inhabited area in the Caucasus, with a population of about twenty-three thousand. It's divided into two parts, Upper Svaneti (Zemo Svaneti) and Lower Svaneti (Kvemo Svaneti), both of which have the most inaccessible and difficult terrains in Georgia. Mestia, the chief town of Upper Svaneti, was not accessible by motor vehicles until 1935, when a footpath was widened with dynamite. Situated 7,220 feet (2,200 m) above sea level in the region of Upper Svaneti, Ushguli,

a community of four villages, is the highest continuously inhabited settlement in Europe. Like many other centers in Svaneti, the village is striking because of the dozens of medieval watchtowers that dot its landscape. The surrounding mountain scenery is superb, with good views of the nearby peaks of Ushba and Shkhara.

In 1996, the United Nations Educational, Scientific and Cultural Organization (UNESCO) designated the Upper Svaneti as a World Heritage Site for its medieval villages and tower houses. World Heritage Sites are examples of cultural and natural heritage considered to be of outstanding value to humanity.

the snows ..." Few roads traverse the Great Caucasus; the scenic Georgian Military Highway that links Georgia to Russia is the best known. Other routes over the mountain range include the Mamison Pass in Racha and the Klukhor Pass in Abkhazia.

CENTRAL LOWLANDS The southern slopes of the Caucasus merge gradually into Georgia's central lowland areas. The Kolkhida lowlands are to the west, spreading from the shores of the Black Sea. Many of Georgia's major

THE GEORGIAN MILITARY HIGHWAY

The 128-mile (206 km) Georgian Military Highway cuts north through the Great Caucasus range to connect Georgia with Russia and beyond. Beginning in Tbilisi, this road crosses the precipitous mountains to reach Vladikavkaz in southern Russia. The route that began as a track used by invaders since the first century BCE became part of the legendary Silk Road trading routes between Europe and East Asia.

For many centuries it was dangerous, and in winter it was often impassable. It rises to an impressive height of 7,983 feet (2,433 m) at the Krestovy Pass, which is actually the lowest and easiest route over the Caucasus. The route offers the traveler fantastic views of the surrounding mountains and river valleys.

Today's Georgian Military Highway was originally built by the Russians to improve communications with their new subject territory. It was completed in 1817 by the Russian regional commander General Alexie Yermelov (1772–1861), on the orders of Tsar Alexander I. The name of the route originates from this time, when the Russians used the road to move troops to aid their conquest of Transcaucasia.

rivers rush down from the slopes of the Great Caucasus across the Kolkhida lowlands to the Black Sea. These include the Kodori, Enguri, and Rioni. The Rioni River is thought to be the Phasis of Greek legend, along which Jason and the Argonauts traveled to capture the Golden Fleece. At one time the lowlands were mostly swampland. A development program that constructed drainage canals and river embankments improved the region, so that it is now an important area for growing subtropical crops such as tea and citrus fruits. The climate in this region is hot and damp.

The Kura River wends through Georgia near Gori.

The Likhi mountain range forms a bridge between the Great and Lesser Caucasus, and marks the division between the east and west of the country. To the west of the Likhi range, the Kartalinian Plain forms an arid plateau, situated between Khashuri and the ancient capital of Mtskheta. This central plateau extends along the Kura River and its tributaries. The Kura River is the longest one in Transcaucasia. It begins in northeast Turkey, passes through central Georgia, and runs the whole length of Azerbaijan before flowing into the Caspian Sea. The easternmost part of Georgia is formed around the Alazani River Valley and the Iori Plateau, both of which are divided by the Gombori mountain range. The Alazani Valley is Georgia's chief grape-growing and winemaking region.

THE LESSER CAUCASUS Southern Georgia is marked by the ranges and plateaus of the Lesser Caucasus that divide Georgia from its southern neighbors, Turkey and Armenia. The highest peak of the Lesser Caucasus is Mount Didi-Abuli (10,830 feet/3,300 m). The mountains, almost completely covered with cedar and beech forests, resemble the temperate rain forests of British Columbia.

REGIONS

Georgia is an ethnically diverse country, so regional identity is important to its various peoples. The country is divided into nine administrative regions; two autonomous republics, Abkhazia and Ajaria; and one autonomous region, South Ossetia. (Since 2008, Abkhazia and South Ossetia have proclaimed themselves to be independent republics, backed by and essentially administrated by Russia.) The administrative regions are Guria, Imereti, Kakheti, Kvemo Kartli, Mtskheta-Mtianeti, Racha-Lechkhumi and Kvemo Svaneti, Samegrelo and Zemo Svaneti, Samtskhe-Javakheti, and Shida Kartli.

These regions are subdivided into sixty-five districts. Historically, Imereti and Samegrelo formed the nucleus of western Georgia, while Kartli and Kakheti formed the rump of eastern Georgia. Regions such as Upper and Lower Svaneti, Khevi, and Khevsureti are mountainous and lightly populated.

CITIES

TBILISI   With a population of 1.1 million, Tbilisi (t-BLI-si), the capital of Georgia, is the country's most populous city. It is a long, narrow city that straddles both banks of the Kura River. The city is built on several hills and is protected on three sides by mountains. Founded in 458 CE by King Vakhtang Gorgasali, Tbilisi was named after some nearby hot sulfur springs. The name Tbilisi means "warm." The city, situated at the crossroads between Asia and Europe, reflects the influences of both continents. Ruled by both Muslims and Christians at different times in its history, Tbilisi has a cosmopolitan, multiethnic character that is reflected in its architecture, which ranges from

This view of Tbilisi shows the new (2010) glass and steel pedestrian Bridge of Peace (*light blue*, center) spanning the Kura River

Batumi is a seaside city on the Black Sea coast.

the Moorish-style Opera House to medieval churches and Baroque Russian architecture. The city's main, tree-lined thoroughfare, Rustaveli Avenue, is named after the thirteenth-century Georgian poet Shota Rustaveli. Georgians have always venerated their poets above other artists. Tbilisi is also an industrial city and accounts for more than 40 percent of the country's industrial output. It has had a subway system since 1966.

BATUMI Now Georgia's second-largest city, Batumi (population 153,000) is the capital of the autonomous region of Ajaria and is Georgia's most important port on the southern Black Sea coast. It began as a port under the Romans and reached its height of prominence in the Middle Ages, but was devastated by the Turks in the sixteenth century. Modern Batumi is a city of parks with subtropical vegetation, a broad stony beach, and high-rise tourist hotels. Despite the town's wet climate, it is a popular holiday resort, especially with Russian tourists.

KUTAISI Situated near the Rioni River in the central lowlands, Kutaisi is the capital of the Imereti region. It has a population of 147,600, making it the third-largest city. Legend has it that the capital city of King Aeëtes, custodian of the Golden Fleece, was situated here. The Rioni River—known in ancient times as the Phasis—is navigable all the way to the Black Sea, and would have allowed Jason and his Argonauts access to it. Kutaisi is known to have existed as a Greek colony in the seventh century BCE, and was the capital of Georgia from 978 to 1122 CE. It contains impressive medieval structures such as the Bagrati Cathedral, Gelati Monastery, which together are a UNESCO World Heritage site; and the Monastery of Montsameta—all built between the tenth and twelfth centuries, the "golden age" of King David the Builder and Queen Tamar.

CLIMATE

Georgia has a varied climate, ranging from subtropical humidity to snow and ice. The Great Caucasus forms a barrier that protects Georgia from cold air from the north, while the west of the country is open to warm, moist air from the Black Sea. Western Georgia has a damp subtropical climate with heavy rainfall all year. The rain is heaviest around Batumi in the south. Winters in the west are mild and warm, and the temperature never falls below 32°F (0°C). Along the Black Sea coast, the temperature rarely falls below 40°F (4°C). Eastern Georgia is cut off from the warm air of the Black Sea by the Likhi mountain range and consequently has a drier, more continental climate. Altitude also exerts an important climatic influence. Most of the Caucasus is above 6,000 feet (1,800 m) and has an Alpine climate, lacking a true summer. Many of eastern Georgia's mountains are over 11,000 feet (3,300 m) above sea level and are covered with snow most of the year.

FLORA AND FAUNA

Georgia's varied landscape has created an unusual diversity of flora. Forests and brush cover more than one-third of the country, and the vegetation varies from east to west. Some flora in western Georgia is subtropical. Alder trees predominate in the swampy coastal areas of the Kolkhida lowlands. Farther inland, where the climate is drier, the forests include oak, chestnut, beech, and liana. The Pitsunda pine can be found in Abkhazia. A grove of these unique trees is protected in a national park on the Pitsunda Cape.

Eastern Georgia has fewer forests and is dominated by grasslands dotted with prickly undergrowth. The lowlands and foothills are forested only along the rivers, especially the Kura, Iori, and Alazani, where oak, poplar, and willow trees can be found. In the higher, wetter regions, juniper, pomegranate, Georgian maple, and pistachio trees grow well. Georgia's unique geographical

PHEASANTS (PHASIANUS COLCHICUS)

Pheasants are indigenous throughout the Caucasus and southeastern Europe. They are larger than quail or partridge, and most are long-tailed birds of the open woodlands and fields, although some prefer grain fields near brushy cover. All pheasants have hoarse calls and a variety of other call-notes. The males of most pheasant species are strikingly colored, while the females are more inconspicuous. Courting males sometimes fight to the death in the presence of hens. Many pheasants are kept in private collections and are also raised for sport in some game reserves. Some species have been brought to the verge of extinction by hunting.

Legend has it that Jason and the Argonauts first introduced pheasants to Greece (and from there to the rest of Europe) when they returned home from their arduous adventures. It is thought that the name pheasant derives from the River Phasis, now called the Rioni River, down which the Argonauts traveled when they escaped from Colchis with the Golden Fleece.

location has resulted in a mixture of European and Asian fauna. There are gazelles, deer, and wild boars in eastern Georgia's lowlands.

The western lowlands of the country have a greater diversity of fauna. A variety of mammals such as moles, squirrels, brown bears, badgers, weasels, deer, wolves, foxes, lynx, mink, and wildcats can be found here. Birds of this region include pheasants, geese, curlews, ducks, cormorants, and woodpeckers, and, during times of migration, pelicans, storks, herons, hawks, and eagle owls.

The Alpine areas of Georgia are inhabited by many species of birds, including the Caucasian jackdaw, black grouse, pheasant, cuckoo, woodpecker, and magpie. Goats and Caucasian antelope can also be found in the mountains, and the rivers are full of trout.

The Black Sea has a rich diversity of sea life, including dolphins, sharks, salmon, herring, dogfish, and swordfish.

A Eurasian lynx sits in a tree.

INTERNET LINKS

https://www.britannica.com/place/Georgia
This encyclopaedia provides a good overview of Georgian geography.

http://census.ge/files/results/Census_release_ENG.pdf
This is an English language overview of the 2014 Georgia population census.

http://whc.unesco.org/en/list/709
This is the UNESCO listing for the Upper Svaneti region of Georgia.

http://whc.unesco.org/en/list/710
This is the UNESCO listing for the Bagrati Cathedral and Gelati Monastery in Kutaisi.

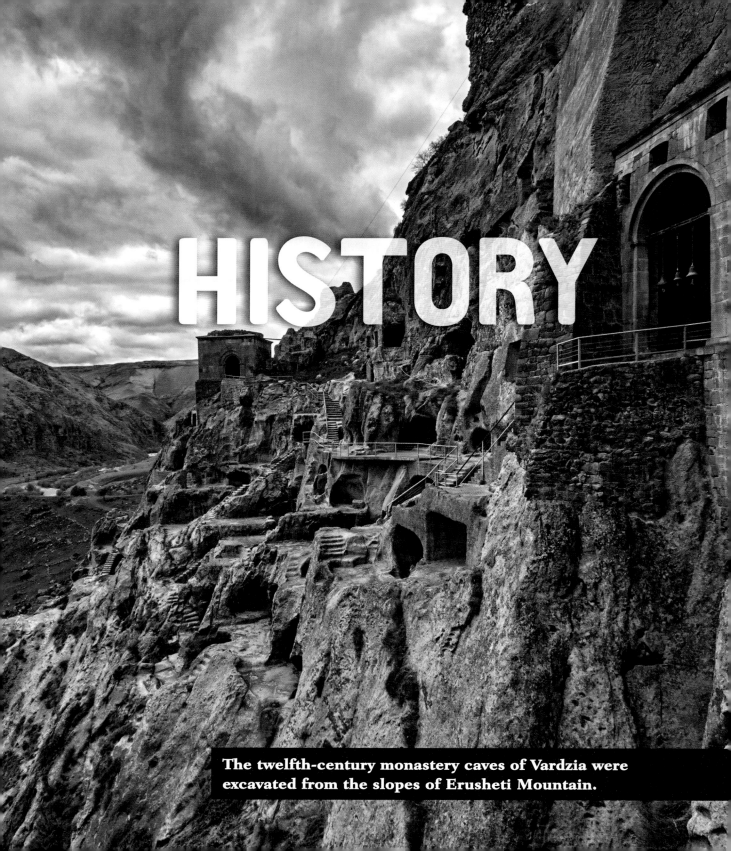

HISTORY

The twelfth-century monastery caves of Vardzia were excavated from the slopes of Erusheti Mountain.

G EORGIA IS A TINY COUNTRY IN A dangerous position. Situated at a geographical crossroads between Europe and Asia, it shares the complicated and turbulent history of the Middle East. Bordered by an enormous and powerful neighbor—which in recent years seems keen on expanding its territory—its continued existence can seem doubtful.

But then, this fiercely independent Caucasian republic has often been dominated by greater neighboring powers—Byzantium, Persia, Turkey, and most recently Russia—all of which have left their marks. Despite these influences, however, Georgia has retained a unique national identity, culture, and language.

EARLY HISTORY

Archaeological excavations and the discovery of cave drawings along the Black Sea coast suggest human habitation around the Middle Paleolithic period (150,000—40,000 BCE). Paleolithic humans lived in caves or earth dugouts and survived mainly by hunting animals and gathering fruits and berries. A Neolithic culture existed in Georgia from 5000 to 4000 BCE. The Neolithic inhabitants were hunters, fishers, and food gatherers.

Bronze Age humans thrived in Georgia between the third and second millennia BCE. It was at about this time that Georgian metallurgy

2

Joseph Stalin, the notoriously cruel Soviet ruler from 1929 to his death in 1953, is arguably Georgia's most famous son. After independence, many Stalin statues throughout the country were torn down, but now some are being replaced. Georgian attitudes toward Stalin are mixed, with some people venerating him as a national hero, while others recall him as a tyrant who murdered his own people.

developed and Georgian metalworkers became the most renowned in the ancient world.

At the end of the third millennium BCE, the Kurgan people invaded the Caucasus from the Eurasian grasslands. Elements of this Kurgan culture fused with the cultures of the local people to form the famous Trialeti culture in the region southwest of Tbilisi. Remarkable finds in Trialeti show that it was inhabited by cattle-raising tribes whose chieftains were people of power and wealth. Burial mounds have been discovered that date from 2100 to 1500 BCE. Many of them contain vessels of gold and silver.

COLCHIS AND GREECE

The historical records of the Assyrians provide the first concrete evidence of the rulers and tribes of Georgia. The western part of Georgia, then known as Colchis, is famous in ancient history and mythology. It was first mentioned in Assyrian records in the twelfth century BCE. From the eighth century BCE on, the place had been visited by the ancient Greeks, who set up colonies and trading stations all around the Black Sea.

Silver coins from Colchis date from the sixth century BCE.

THE IBERIANS

Around 730 BCE, the Cimmerians and Scythians from the north attacked Georgia and occupied Colchis and much of the Caucasus. Their invasions scattered many of the ancestral tribes of Georgia into the more remote mountain regions, and pushed some of them into the Persian sphere of influence. However, the Tibareni and Mushki tribes managed to reestablish themselves in eastern Georgia by the time Alexander the Great of Macedonia crushed the Persians at the Battle of Arbela in 331 BCE. The two tribes then merged with local tribes to form the kingdom of Iberia—in Georgia, called the ancient kingdom of Kartli—with its capital at Mtskheta. (This kingdom is also sometimes called "Caucasian Iberia" so as not to confuse it with the Iberian Peninsula, also called Iberia, in Western Europe.)

Here, for the first time, a common Georgian language was developed, and Mtskheta, situated 20 miles (32 km) north of modern-day Tbilisi, thrived at the crossroads of a busy trade route that linked Greece to the west with India and China to the east.

In 66 BCE, the Romans, under the command of Pompey, conquered Iberia. The resulting Roman influence brought many advantages to the Iberians, including new roads and increased trade with the rest of the Roman Empire. Soon Iberia established such good relations with the Romans that Iberia was considered an ally rather than a subject state.

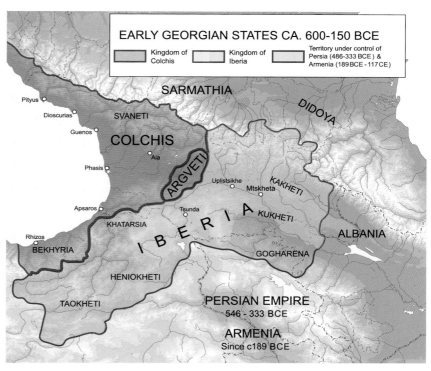

EARLY GEORGIAN STATES CA. 600-150 BCE

Kingdom of Colchis

Kingdom of Iberia

Territory under control of Persia (486-333 BCE) & Armenia (189 BCE - 117 CE)

SARMATHIA

DIDOYA

Pityus

Dioscurias

SVANETI

Guenos

COLCHIS

Aia

Phasis

ARGVETI

Uplistsikhe

Mtskheta

KAKHETI

Apsaros

Tsunda

I B E R I A

KUKHETI

KHATARSIA

Rhizos

BEKHYRIA

ALBANIA

GOGHARENA

HENIOKHETI

PERSIAN EMPIRE
546 - 333 BCE

TAOKHETI

ARMENIA
Since c189 BCE

This map shows the ancient kingdoms of Georgia. Silver coins from Colchis date from the sixth century BCE.

The earliest version of this legend was told by Apollonius Rhodius in his epic poem Argonautica, composed in the third century BCE. Greek geographer Strabo (63 BCE–23 CE) also tells of the Golden Fleece in his literary work Geography. *Many details in the Argonautica have since been supported by archaeological evidence, suggesting that the Argonauts' journey may be more than just a legend.*

According to the story, a Greek prince named Jason set out with a band of fifty men in a ship called the Argo *to find the fabled Golden Fleece—the fleece of the gold-haired winged ram, a symbol of authority and kingship. His uncle, Pelias, had usurped the throne belonging to his father, and Jason could only regain his rightful crown by proving his bravery. In the search for the Golden Fleece, the Argonauts encountered many dangers during a long and eventful journey that finally took them to Colchis.*

There Aeëtes, the Colchian king, refused to give up the Golden Fleece unless Jason went through several trials. First he had to tame the king's fire-snorting bulls and yoke them to a plow, which Jason achieved through strength and cunning. Next he had to plow a field and plant a helmet full of dragon's teeth, each of which sprang up into armed warriors, whom he then had to defeat. Aeëtes's daughter Medea, a sorceress who had fallen in love with Jason, stepped in to help. She advised him to throw a stone among the warriors, causing confusion so that they turned in anger upon one another and fought to the death, leaving Jason victorious.

Aeëtes, however, still refused to part with the Golden Fleece, which was being guarded by an ever-watchful dragon. Once again Medea went to Jason's aid. She guided him to the Fleece and cast a spell on the dragon, causing it to fall asleep. This allowed Jason to escape in the Argo *with both the Golden Fleece and Medea.*

CONVERSION TO CHRISTIANITY

The Iberians embraced Christianity in 330 CE during the reign of the Roman Emperor Constantine the Great. The conversion is attributed to Saint Nino, a woman who was said to possess healing powers. Political conditions favored the adoption of the new religion—it was the official creed of the still-powerful Romans, and neighboring Armenia had converted thirty years earlier. In the fifth century CE, King Vakhtang Gorgasali (reigned 446—510) strengthened the Iberian Church by establishing an independent bishop at Mtskheta, which remains the center of the Georgian Orthodox Church today. The king also moved his capital to Tbilisi in 458, thus founding the capital city.

To the west of Iberia, Lazica—a kingdom that had sprung up from the ruins of Colchis—adopted Christianity in the sixth century. For much of the sixth and seventh centuries, Lazica and Iberia found themselves at the center of a power struggle between Byzantium to the west and Persia to the east. The struggle ended when the Arabs, inspired by the new Islamic faith, swept through Persia and the entire region, capturing Tbilisi in 645.

ARAB DOMINATION

The Arabs were not interested in colonizing Georgia, and Georgian culture and Christian religion were allowed to flourish. Georgian princes were allowed to rule, but under Arab supervision. Tbilisi soon became the center of several important international trade routes that transported goods from Russia, Daghestan, and the Middle East.

In the ninth century the Bagratid clan came into prominence. The Bagratids would unite Georgia under a single crown and hold power for the next one thousand years. Their rule ended only with Russian annexation in 1801. The first Bagratid ruler, King Ashot I (reigned 813—830), was appointed ruler of much of southern Georgia. Under King Bagrat III (reigned 975—1014), the eastern and western parts of Georgia became unified for the first time. It is only from this time that Georgia can be referred to as the single entity we know of today. Under King Bagrat IV (reigned 1027—1072), Georgia became one of the most powerful states in the Caucasus.

DAVID THE BUILDER

A statue of David the Builder stands before the Metekhi Church of Virgin Mary in Tbilisi.

In the eleventh century the Seljuk Turks pushed westward, capturing Persia and Armenia and invading Byzantium. The Byzantine Army was crushed at Manzikert in 1071. Later the son of King Bagrat IV, King Giorgi II, reigned from 1072 until 1089, when, unable to deal with the onslaught of the Turks, he abdicated the throne. His sixteen-year-old son, David (1073—1125), took over.

Under King David, who was known as The Builder, national unity was restored, and trade, culture, and religion flourished. King David resisted the Turks, winning many brilliant victories between 1110 and 1122, and defeating the Turks decisively at the Battle of Didgori in 1121. Tbilisi was recaptured from the Turks in 1122. The king's humane treatment of the Turkish Muslim population set a standard of tolerance in his multiethnic kingdom.

King David also managed to extend Georgia's territory as far as the Caspian Sea, and he captured parts of Armenia as well. His campaigns were indirectly aided by the timely arrival of the European Crusaders in Palestine. The Crusaders captured the Holy Land in 1099 and were a constant threat to the Islamic world over the next few centuries, allowing Georgia to develop its own culture and reinforce and extend its borders without Arab interference. (The term Holy Land generally refers to Israel and the historic geographical region of Palestine. It concerns the areas that hold significant religious importance to the three monotheistic Abrahamic religions: Judaism, Christianity, and Islam.)

QUEEN TAMAR

The great works of King David were continued by his great-granddaughter, Queen Tamar (reigned 1184—1212). Christian culture flourished, and many religious buildings were constructed, among them the Vardzia Caves. With the fall of the Byzantine Empire to the Muslims in 1204, Queen Tamar was able to extend the boundaries of Georgia westward along the Black Sea coast and create the independent empire of Trebizond. Under Queen Tamar the Georgian feudal system reached its zenith and the virtues of chivalry and honor were celebrated in Shota Rustaveli's (1172—1216) epic romance, *The Knight in the Panther's Skin*.

THE MONGOL YOKE

The Mongol invasion of Transcaucasia in 1220 brought Georgia's "golden age" to an end. Led by Genghis Khan, the Mongols swept across much of Asia and eventually threatened the borders of Europe. The Mongols were an aggressive, well-armed, and well-trained army of horsemen who were notorious for their cruelty and bravery. Queen Tamar's heir, King Giorgi IV Lasha (reigned 1213—1222), was killed in a battle against the Mongols. The Mongols dominated Georgia for the next century, taxing the Georgians heavily.

King Giorgi V (reigned 1314—1346), who was called "The Brilliant," took advantage of weakening Mongol power to regain Georgian independence. Unfortunately the Central Asian conqueror, Tamerlane (1336—1405), in the course of his campaigns against the Turks and Persians, caused much havoc and destruction from which the kingdom never fully recovered. Georgia was overrun on eight consecutive occasions; towns and churches were ruined, and the people fled to the hills.

OTTOMAN TURKEY AND SAFAVID PERSIA

In 1453 the Ottoman Turks captured Constantinople, isolating Georgia from European Christendom. At the end of the fifteenth century the rise of the Safavid Persians posed a further threat to Georgia, which found itself caught once more between two expanding empires to the east and west. Both the Turks and Persians encroached upon Georgian territory until, in the Peace of Amasia in 1555, Georgia was divided into spheres of influence—the Turks controlled western Georgia while the Persians controlled the eastern part. The Georgians were powerless to resist.

In 1578 the Turks overran the whole of Transcaucasia, but were subsequently driven out by the Persian Shah Abbas I (reigned 1557—1628). The Georgian people were heavily persecuted for their Christian beliefs, and many were deported to distant regions of Persia (present-day Iran), where their descendants can still be found today. Queen Ketevan of Kakheti was given the choice of abandoning the Christian faith and entering the shah's harem, or suffering a cruel martyrdom. She chose to die for her faith, and is numbered among the saints of the Georgian Church. For the next two hundred years the kings of Kartli, as eastern Georgia was then known, ruled only through the will of the Persian shahs.

RUSSIAN ANNEXATION

In the early eighteenth century the Bagratid kings Taimuraz II (reigned 1744—1762) and Heraclius II (reigned 1762—1798) were able to rebuild Georgia in its own image, not Persia's. Persian power was waning, and the Russians were expanding into Transcaucasia. Nevertheless Persian-backed Muslim raiders from north of the Caucasus and Daghestan had a crippling effect on Georgian trade and industry. It is estimated that the population of Georgia might have been reduced by as much as half by the end of the eighteenth century because of these attacks. King Heraclius II, convinced that his isolated Christian kingdom could not hold out against an assortment of Muslim enemies, sought the aid of Christian Russia.

In 1783 Russia and Georgia signed the Treaty of Georgievsk. Under the agreement Georgia became a Russian protectorate, renouncing all dependence on Persia. Despite Russian promises of protection, Tbilisi was sacked again in 1795 by the Persians, and fifty thousand of its inhabitants were killed. Heraclius II, the seventy-five-year-old king, fought in the battle and narrowly escaped capture. He died in 1798.

In 1800 Heraclius II's son, the invalid King Giorgi XII, decided to hand over the kingdom to the care of the Russians unconditionally in exchange for their full protection. The king died that same year. He was the last ruler of the thousand-year-old Bagratid Dynasty. In 1801 the Russian Tsar

Alexander I confirmed that Kartli and Kakheti were a part of the Russian Empire and abolished the Bagratid monarchy. The western realm (Imereti) ruled by Solomon II continued until 1810, only to meet the same fate.

GEORGIA UNDER THE CZARS

The Treaty of Georgievsk, 1783, shows Heraclius II's signature and seal.

Under Czar Alexander I, the Russians continued their expansion into the Caucasus, waging war against the Turks, Persians, and the Lezgian tribesmen of Daghestan. Russian power brought stability to Georgia, and under the guidance of the gifted and enlightened Russian viceroy Michael Vorontsov (1782—1856), industry and trade prospered, and communications improved. In 1872 a railway was built to link Tbilisi with Poti, and Russian and Western entrepreneurs developed plantations.

With increased communication, however, came change. The Russian social administration replaced the old Georgian feudal system, and Russian education and culture became widespread. Many Georgian intellectuals reacted against Russian influence. The "Men of the 1860s" were a group of radicals and social activists, full of the new social democratic ideals that were then current in Europe. Although tsarist Russia did not permit any organized political activity, social issues were debated in journals and local assemblies, and through works of fiction.

The 1890s saw the appearance of a new group of radicals who had absorbed the political ideals of Karl Marx, a revolutionary Communist from Germany, while studying abroad. They were called the *tergdaleulni* (terg-dal-e-UL-ni), meaning "those who had drunk from the river Terek," an act that symbolized their going out into the world, beyond the boundaries of Georgia.

Perhaps the most famous and notorious Georgian of modern times, Stalin was born in Gori, Inner Kartli. Originally christened Joseph Vissarionovich Dzhugashvili, he adopted the name Stalin, meaning "man of steel" in Russian, when he entered revolutionary politics. Stalin's family was poor and his father was a drunkard. Despite great hardship,

his mother succeeded in sending Joseph to an Orthodox seminary in Tbilisi, where he trained for the priesthood. He was expelled in 1899; it is suspected that this was because he was propagating Marxism.

Although he was anti-czarist, Stalin was never a nationalist. He did not believe that Georgia's salvation lay in independence, but rather in becoming part of a larger political structure. He became active in Georgia's revolutionary underground. He was arrested and imprisoned many times and exiled to Siberia twice by the tsarist authorities. He became friends with Lenin and was at the forefront of the 1917 Bolshevik Revolution. When Lenin died in 1924, Stalin had so much power that he was able to isolate and disgrace his political rivals. In 1928 he exiled his main political rival, Leon Trotsky (1879–1940), and gained absolute control of the Communist Party.

Stalin was a cruel, ruthless, and dictatorial ruler who was responsible for the imprisonment or death of many millions of people in the Soviet Union through forced collectivization and political purges in the 1930s. It is estimated that as many as twenty million Soviet citizens died as a result of his policies. Nevertheless he gained a reputation as a great war leader, leading the Soviet Union to victory over the Germans in World War II. He died on March 5, 1953, under mysterious circumstances, probably from a brain hemorrhage.

The leader of this group was Noe Zhordania (1868—1953). Another prominent member was Joseph Dzhugashvili, better known as Joseph Stalin.

WAR AND REVOLUTION A failed 1905 revolution in Russia led to social unrest and industrial strikes in Georgia. These were brutally suppressed by Cossacks, a group in southern Russia that fought for the tsarist army. In 1914 Russia entered World War I, fighting against the Germans and Austrians. The Russian Army collapsed in 1917, amid economic disintegration, severe food shortages, and social upheaval at home. This was followed by one of the twentieth century's most momentous events: the Russian Revolution, which began in November 1917. Under the leadership of Vladimir Lenin (1870—1924), the Bolsheviks, a political group which ultimately became the Communist Party of the Soviet Union, seized power.

In Georgia the power vacuum was filled by the Social Democratic Party, led by Noe Zhordania. The country regained its autonomy for the first time in 117 years and maintained a neutral stance throughout the Russian civil war, from 1917 to 1920, but its independence was short-lived. In February 1921, following victories throughout Russia, the Bolshevik Eleventh Red Army marched into Georgia, driving Zhordania and his government into exile. Georgia was once more in the grip of its more powerful neighbor.

SOVIET GEORGIA

Georgia was initially incorporated into the Transcaucasian Soviet Federated Republic in 1922, along with Armenia and Azerbaijan. The Georgian Social Democrats, still popular despite their earlier defeat, organized a rebellion in 1924 that was put down by the Red Army. Seven thousand people were executed, and Soviet rule was finally established in Georgia.

In 1936 Georgia became one of the fifteen republics of the Soviet Union. Joseph Stalin, a native Georgian, ruled the Soviet Union from 1928 to 1953. Despite the fact that he and his chief of police, Lavrenti Beria (1899—1953), were Georgians, Stalin treated his homeland harshly.

During World War II (1939—1945), the Georgians helped defend the Soviet Union against the German invasion of the northern Caucasus. German paratroopers were dropped into Georgia to aid the German advance, but they were promptly caught by the local militia. The German advance was thus stemmed.

Soviet economic policy forced the collectivization—a policy adopted by the Soviet government and pursued most intensively between 1929 and 1933 to transform traditional agriculture in the Soviet Union and to reduce the economic power of the prosperous peasants—of all agricultural workers, as had happened throughout the Soviet Union. Georgia was converted from a largely agricultural economy into an industrial and urban society.

Following Stalin's death in 1953, a freewheeling "second economy" developed, providing goods and services that were not available in the planned state economy. Far from the center of power in Moscow, most Georgians were able to grow their own crops privately and run their own cottage industries; they remain fundamental to the economy and lifestyle even today. Older Georgians still look back to the 1960s and 1970s with great nostalgia. It was a time of public order, peace, and high standards of living.

A veteran lays flowers at the Unknown Soldier Tomb memorial in Tbilisi on Victory Day in 2016, marking the anniversary of the Soviet Union's victory over Nazi Germany in World War II.

INDEPENDENCE

In the late 1980s, the Soviet Union underwent fundamental political and social changes under the leadership of Mikhail Gorbachev (b. 1931). In the new atmosphere of *glasnost* (openness), political and social freedoms were reinstated.

In April 1989 demonstrations held in Tbilisi to demand independence were brutally suppressed by Soviet special troops, and twenty civilians were killed. After the tragic event, however, the massacre was reported by the Soviet authorities to have been a mistake. Soviet President Gorbachev had not ordered the suppression; the decision had been made by the local government and army commanders. It was partly due to this event that the Soviets began to lose control over Georgia: Anti-Soviet sentiment was fueled by the suppression, and this speeded up the move toward independence. There was little that the Soviet authorities could do other than launch a full military invasion, which would have been highly impractical and unpopular in the unstable social and political climate of the time.

Soon new political parties appeared. Free elections held in 1990 were won by a coalition called the Round Table, led by a former dissident named Zviad Gamsakhurdia (1939—1994). Georgia was declared independent on April 9, 1991, and Gamsakhurdia was elected president of the new republic. His authoritarian rule made him unpopular, however. Civil war broke out in late 1991, and a military council deposed him in 1992. The military council soon handed power to a state council made up of various political parties that were headed by Eduard Shevardnadze (b. 1928). Shevardnadze had served as Soviet foreign minister under Gorbachev. Despite terrorist attempts to kill him in August 1995, elections held in November of that same year confirmed him as president for five years. In 2000 he would emerge victorious yet again in the presidential elections.

The Soviet Union disintegrated in 1991, and the Commonwealth of Independent States (CIS) was formed, consisting of fifteen newly independent countries of the former Soviet Union. Georgia joined the CIS in 1993, but withdrew in August 2009 following the Russia-Georgia War of 2008.

BREAKAWAY REGIONS

Life for independent Georgia has not been peaceful or trouble-free, and the nation still has much to do in order to establish stability in one of the most volatile regions in the world. In 1992, shortly after the country achieved its independence, the people of the South Ossetia province voted, in an unofficial referendum, in favor of their own independence from Georgia. They sought unification with North Ossetia, which lies in Russia. Likewise, that same year, separatists in Abkhazia began fighting Georgia government troops. The Russian government supported both provinces and sent peacekeepers to the regions as part of a ceasefire agreement. Nevertheless, Georgia continued to consider the provinces its sovereign territory.

Tensions, including sporadic clashes, came to a head in 2008 when it appeared that Russia sent soldiers to South Ossetia and Georgian government suspected Moscow was preparing to annex the province. Georgian troops tried to retake South Ossetia by force, prompting a full-blown military conflict that went on for five days. The hostilities, sometimes called the Russo-Georgian

This map shows the extensive border that Georgia shares with Russia, and where the breakaway regions are located.

War of 2008, claimed hundreds of lives on all sides, including civilians, and injured thousands more.

Since then, the breakaway regions have declared independence, with immediate Russian recognition. Both are heavily dependent on Russia, which effectively controls them. Recent moves by Russia, such as placing barbed wire and armed guards at the regions' borders with Georgia, suggest that Moscow intends to absorb the regions into Russia.

Georgia considers Abkhazia and South Ossetia to be its own sovereign territory held under Russian military occupation. Most countries in the international community agree, including the EU, NATO, and the United States, but the impasse is unlikely to hang in limbo for long. In 2015, Russia began moving the South Ossetian—Georgian border further into Georgia, with no discussion, getting ever closer to the main road linking the west and east of the country.

INTERNET LINKS

http://www.bbc.com/news/world-europe-17303471
The BBC News provides a timeline of events in Georgian history.

http://www.bbc.com/news/world-europe-21656615
This article discusses Georgians' divided attitude toward Joseph Stalin.

https://www.britannica.com/place/Georgia/Cultural-life#toc214120
Britannica offers a Georgian history chapter with several maps.

http://www.lonelyplanet.com/georgia/history
This site covers Georgia's history from ancient times to about 2008.

GOVERNMENT

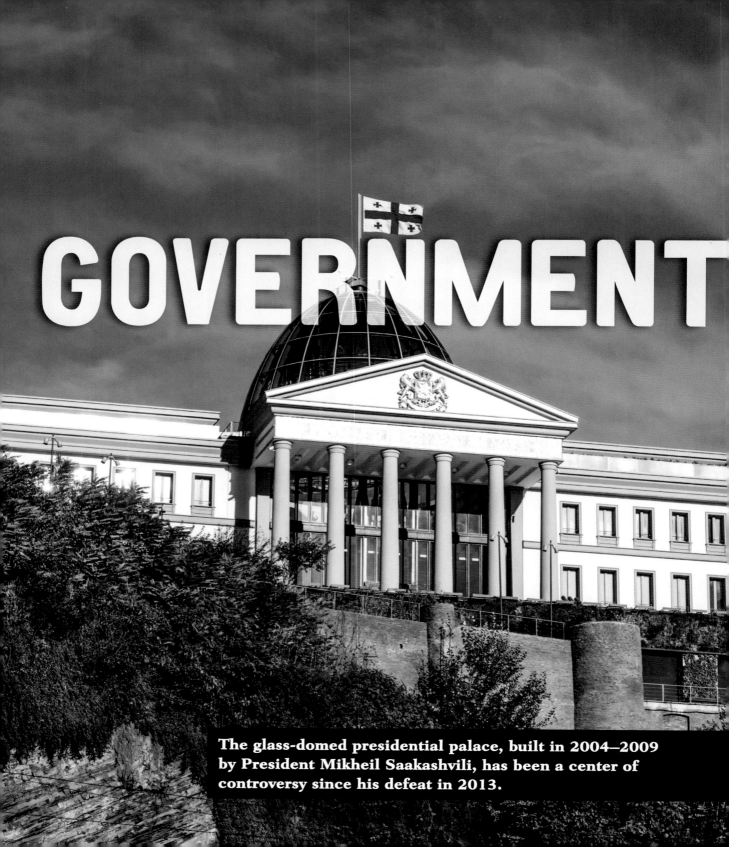

The glass-domed presidential palace, built in 2004–2009 by President Mikheil Saakashvili, has been a center of controversy since his defeat in 2013.

F OR SEVENTY YEARS, GEORGIA WAS A part of the Soviet Union and had no independent government of its own. A Georgian parliament did exist— the Georgian Supreme Soviet—but as the national branch of the Communist Party, it could only implement decisions that were made centrally by the Communist Party leaders in Moscow.

Amid the disintegration of the Soviet Union, free elections were held in 1990 and Zviad Gamsakhurdia emerged victorious. However, his dictatorial methods led to his swift exit from power in early 1992. Eduard Shevardnadze (1928—2014), the chairperson of the state council, was temporarily elected and an emergency constitution passed. Gamsakhurdia continued his opposition to the new government before dying under mysterious circumstances in early 1994.

Shevardnadze was democratically elected as Georgia's leader in presidential elections held on November 5, 1995, and was re-elected in 2000. A shrewd politician with vast international experience, he sought to modernize Georgia and forge closer economic ties with the West and the other newly independent republics in the Caucasus and Central Asia. Having served as foreign minister in Mikhail Gorbachev's Soviet administration during the 1980s, his international stature ensured that Georgia's problems were gaining attention from other world leaders.

The medieval flag of Georgia, also known as the Five-Cross Flag, was adopted in 2004. It is a white rectangle with a single red cross in the center surrounded by four smaller crosses, one in each quadrant. The symbolism is uncertain, though there are many interpretations. The design dates to a fourteenth-century Kingdom of Georgia banner.

Between 1992 and 1993, Abkhzia and South Ossetia achieved *de facto* independence from Georgia amid extensive interethnic violence and wars. Abkhaz separatists forced more than 250,000 Georgians, including Chechens, to leave Abkhazia.

ROSE REVOLUTION

Shevardnadze resigned following widespread allegations of ballot fraud in the parliamentary election of November 2003. Thousands of peaceful protesters carried roses through the streets of Tbilisi. For twenty days, people protested, triggering new presidential and parliamentary elections. This became known as the Rose Revolution, which marked the end of Soviet leadership in Georgia, and a turn toward a pro-Western policy stance. Georgia now looked away from Russia and toward Europe for its future.

THE SAAKASHVILI PRESIDENCY

Former Georgian President Mikheil Saakashvili gives an anti-corruption speech in Ukraine in 2016.

Mikheil Saakashvili (b. 1967) of the National Movement came to power in January 2004. At the age of thirty-five, Saakashvili became Europe's youngest president. A United States—educated lawyer and former justice minister, the new president spared no time in reforming Georgia's military, bringing it closer to the standards required to become a member of the North Atlantic Treaty Organization (NATO), an organization of North American and European nations for the purpose of mutual military aide. The new president was reelected in early elections in 2008, but by then he had acquired more political enemies. Critics accused him of heavy-handedness against opposition.

During Saakashvili's administration, Georgian relations with Russia soured and tensions rose. In August 2008, they came to a head over the breakaway region of South Ossetia, which aligned itself with Russia. Georgia's attempt to retake South Ossetia militarily ended in a humiliating defeat. In addition, the president was accused of election fraud and protests against him spread across the country. In 2012, Saakashvili's party was defeated in parliamentary elections and, barred from seeking a third presidential term, Saakashvili left the country.

In 2105, he gave up his Georgian citizenship, became a Ukrainian citizen, and soon became the governor of Odessa, Ukraine. He resigned that post less than a year later, citing corruption in Ukraine.

GEORGIAN DREAM

In 2013, the Georgian Dream Party coalition was victorious in the elections, which brought in Giorgi Margvelashvili (b. 1969) as president and Giorgi Kvirikashvili (b. 1967) as prime minister. The coalition itself represents six parties with widely diverse ideological positions, brought together by their opposition to former President Saakashvili. The parties' continued alliance, therefore, remains to be seen. Meanwhile, the country's new leaders have pledged to continue on the path to cementing Western alliances, and are wary of Russian aggression.

In 2017, Prime Minister Giorgi Kvirikashvili holds a press conference.

THE REPUBLIC

Officially, if no longer in actuality, the Georgian republic includes two autonomous republics and one autonomous region: the Abkhazian Autonomous Republic, the Ajarian Autonomous Republic, and the South Ossetian Autonomous Region. These regions were originally formed by the Soviet administration as semi-independent homelands for ethnic minorities.

They had limited self-government, but proved to be hotbeds of ethnic tension and conflict for the fledgling Georgian republic. They are no longer under the control of the Georgian government, however, the United States and many other countries still recognize the breakaway regions of Abkhazia and South Ossetia as parts of Georgia. Russia and its allies do not.

THE CONSTITUTION

Prior to the elections in 1995, a new constitution was drawn up, based on many of the main principles of the country's 1921 constitution. The new constitution confirmed Georgia as a democratic state in which all citizens are equal. The constitution protects basic human rights such as freedom of speech and thought, freedom of religious practice, and the freedom to own property.

Amendments in 2010 reduced the powers of the president and shifted power to the prime minister and the government. It went into force in 2013, upon the inauguration of Giorgi Margvelashvili as president.

EXECUTIVE BRANCH

The president, as head of state, is elected by absolute majority popular vote—in two rounds if needed—for a term of five years and cannot serve more than two terms. He or she chooses a Council of Ministers (also known as a cabinet) and, along with the ministers, holds supreme executive power. The next election is to be held in October 2018.

The prime minister, as head of government, is nominated by Parliament and appointed by the president.

President Giorgi Margvelashvili is inaugurated on November 17, 2013, in Tbilisi.

THE MKHEDRIONI

Before 1991, Georgia's security was provided by the Soviet Army, in which many Georgians served as conscripts. Following independence, two distinct military groups emerged in Georgia. The National Guard was formed to support the government, while a paramilitary group called the Mkhedrioni (m-ked-RIO-ni), led by Dzahba (or Jaba)

Ioseliani (1926–2003), was formed to fight against the secessionist Abkhazians. However, the Mkhedrioni, numbering seven thousand men, soon developed into an independent force that answered only to Ioseliani.

New president Edouard Shevardnadze was unable to control these groups when he first came to power in 1992, and they operated with brutality, like a private army, against Abkhazians and their supporters. In 1995, the Mkhedrioni was implicated in an attempt to assassinate Shevardnadze. The group was subsequently banned, and Ioseliani was imprisoned. Nevertheless, the group continued to operate in the shadows, and was suspected of being deeply involved in organized crime while stoking political violence and launching guerrilla attacks against Abkhazia.

When Ioseliani was released from prison in 2000, he announced his intention to run for the presidency, but died of a heart attack in 2003 at age seventy-six.

LEGISLATIVE BRANCH

The Georgian parliament is a unicameral (one-house) body consisting of 150 members—73 are directly elected to single-member seats by a simple majority vote, and 77 are elected by proportional representation from party lists. Each member is elected for a four-year period. The next election is to be held in 2020.

Ajaria (also spelled Adjara or Adjaria) has been Georgia's least troubled self-governing region since independence, and has not seen the extensive and bloody conflicts experienced in Abkhazia and South Ossetia. Despite their ethnic Georgian origin, the Ajarians retain a strong sense of separate identity, mainly because of their adherence to Islam. Most Georgians in the region converted to Islam during the long period of Ottoman rule.

Ajaria did not become a part of the Russian Empire until as late as 1878, and it was granted autonomy by Soviet Russia as part of an agreement with Muslim Turkey in 1921. Following the breakup of the Soviet Union, many Christian Georgians regarded Muslim Ajaria's autonomy as a threat to a unified Georgian nation. Tensions escalated in 1991 when Georgia's first president, Zviad Gamsakhurdia, announced his intention to end Ajaria's autonomous status. Mass demonstrations took place in Batumi, and when elections were held in 1991, parties in favor of Ajarian autonomy swept the board.

After 1991 Aslan Abishidze ran the region virtually as a personal fiefdom. Tbilisi effectively lost administrative control of Ajaria, although the Ajarian leadership had made it clear that it wished to remain part of Georgia. Eduard Shevardnadze attempted to appease the Ajarians and praised them as a model of stability in a turbulent part of the world.

Following the Rose Revolution, however, a major crisis arose when the new Saakashvili government sought to restore central authority over Ajaria. Foreign governments and international organizations appealed to both sides to exercise restraint and resolve their differences peacefully. Abishidze resigned as leader of Ajaria on May 5, 2004, and was replaced by a succession of leaders. In 2016, Zurab Patradze became the latest chairman of the government of the Autonomous Republic of Ajaria.

Economically, Ajaria has proven to be one of Georgia's most successful regions. The Ajarians have not been affected by the conflicts that have disrupted so much of Georgian life, and cross-border trade with fellow Muslims in Turkey is flourishing.

Parliament and other main government ministries are situated in the Government House of the Republic of Georgia, in the center of Tbilisi. Citizens must be at least eighteen years old to vote in national elections, and twenty-five years old to run as deputies.

JUDICIAL BRANCH

The Supreme Court is the highest court, with the number of judges determined by the president. These judges are nominated by the president and appointed by the parliament for a term of at least ten years.

A Constitutional Court also exists, made up of nine judges. They are selected by the Justice Council of Georgia, a twelve-member consultative body of high-level judges, and then appointed by the president. They serve for ten years.

In addition, there are regional and district courts and a Court of Appeal.

The breakaway Abkhazian and Ajarian autonomous republics each have a separate supreme court and system of lower courts.

INTERNET LINKS

http://www.bbc.com/news/world-europe-17301647
Find profiles of Georgia's leaders on this site.

https://www.cia.gov/library/publications/the-world-factbook/geos/gg.html
The CIA World Factbook provides up-to-date information on Georgia and its government.

http://csb.gov.ge/uploads/2081806.pdf
A PDF of Georgia's current constitution is available in English.

http://gov.ge/index.php?lang_id=ENG
This is the official Government of Georgia page in English.

ECONOMY

Bills and coins of the Georgian currency, the lari.

4

ECONOMICALLY, THINGS ARE looking up for Georgia. The bad old days of the 1990s, the first decade of independence, are mostly a memory. The country was on its own, with its Soviet supports pulled out from under it. It was transitioning away from the old, centrally-planned economic system to a market system, and naturally things were extremely uncertain at first. Unemployment rose sharply, and food prices reached astronomical levels. In 1993—one of the worst years for Georgia, both politically and economically—just about everyone was poor. About 80 percent of the people were living below the official poverty line.

However, things have improved since then, though they have been rocky at times. Georgia's economy grew by more than 10 percent in 2006—2007, based on vigorous foreign investment and robust government spending. Then the global recession hit in tandem with the August 2008 conflict with Russia, and things went south for a while.

In mid-2014, Georgia signed an association agreement with the European Union, paving the way to free trade and visa-free travel.

The economy rebounded from 2010–2016, but has not recovered fully. In 2010, the percentage of people living below the poverty line was 9.2 percent. By 2016 the unemployment rate had been reduced to 12.1 percent—which is still relatively high—and about two million people were in the workforce.

Now the largest share of Georgia's gross domestic product (GDP) is produced by the service sector. This is followed by industries, including the mining of manganese, copper, and gold; and smaller scale industries producing alcoholic and nonalcoholic beverages, metals, machinery, and chemicals. Agriculture products include grapes, citrus fruits, and hazelnuts.

FROM PUBLIC TO PRIVATE OWNERSHIP

Under the Soviet system, the Georgian economy was run on socialist principles—public ownership of the means of production (farms, offices, factories, and industry) coupled with a centralized, state-planned economy. In 1994 the government began a campaign of mass privatization, followed in 1996 by legislation that allowed for the private ownership of land and regulations for the operation of commercial banks. During the Soviet era the government fixed prices of essential goods and services. Today the costs of food, gas, electricity, transportation, and communications are controlled by market forces and are on a par with world levels.

A man stands at a currency exchange machine in Tbilisi in 2016.

TAXES AND CORRUPTION

The Georgian government is making progress in reforming the tax code, enforcing taxes, and cracking down on corruption. The country has long suffered from a chronic failure to collect tax revenues, which naturally hurt its

Gross domestic product (GDP) is a measure of a country's total production. The number reflects the total value of goods and services produced over a specific time period— typically one year. Economists use it to find out if a country's economy is growing or contracting. Growth is good, while a falling GDP means trouble. Dividing the GDP by the number of people in the country determines the GDP per capita. This number provides an indication of a country's average standard of living—the higher the better.

ability to invest in infrastructure, health, education, and a wide range of other support and improvement programs. However, since 2004, it has simplified the tax code, improved tax administration, increased tax enforcement, and cracked down on petty corruption. All this has led to higher revenues.

The World Bank has noticed the government's anti-corruption efforts. Since 2012, the new Georgian Dream-led government has continued the Saakashvili administration's low-regulation, low-tax, free market policies, while carefully increasing social spending. It has also strengthened the nation's anti-trust policy, and amended its labor code to comply with International Labor Standards.

AGRICULTURE

Approximately 12 percent of the land in Georgia is used for agriculture. Under the Soviet system the traditional, small family farms and estates of the Georgian nobility were replaced by government-run collective farms that required many workers. Today most of these farms have been privatized and divided into smaller units for private ownership.

Garden plots have traditionally been popular in Georgia. Under the Soviet system they were viewed as valuable sources of extra income for their owners. Back then, as much as 40 percent of Georgia's entire agricultural output was provided by produce from private plots.

A farming family gathers grapes from their vineyard in the village of Kachreti.

The country's exceptionally sunny climate promotes the growing of subtropical crops. Tea and citrus fruits are grown in Ajaria, Guria, Samegrelo, Imereti, and Abkhazia. Wine grapes, tobacco, olives, figs, almonds, apples, pears, and some grains and sugar beets are also grown throughout western Georgia. Reclamation of swampy lowlands around the mouth of the Rioni River added fertile land for the production of tea, citrus fruit, grapes, tobacco, and silk.

The Alazani Valley in Kakheti is recognized as the country's premier winemaking region. Before 1991 Georgia was the leading producer of table wines in the Soviet Union. Plants such as geraniums, roses, jasmine, and basil thrive here and are used by the perfume industry.

In the highland areas and on the Kartalinian Plain, the climate favors crops such as barley, oats, apples, plums, and cherries, as well as sheep grazing. Mountainous areas such as Upper Svaneti are used mainly for sheep and goat farming. About half of the working population is employed in the agricultural industry, making it the largest employer in the country. However, it only accounts for about 9.2 percent of Georgia's GDP.

MINERAL WEALTH

Georgia is rich in nonferrous metals, including copper, lead, zinc, and some deposits of silver and gold. There are about three hundred known mineral ores in the republic, of which only half are currently being exploited. There are substantial reserves of clay that can be used to make cement and other building products. Since antiquity Georgia has been famous for its metallurgy. The area around Kutaisi is rich in manganese deposits, a mineral used to make high-grade steel. Georgia's main industrial center is Rustavi, located 20 miles (32 km) southeast of Tbilisi. Rustavi is a typical industrial town with iron and steel mills and various chemical plants. Here laminated sheet iron and seamless pipe products are made.

Throughout Georgia factories produce diverse goods such as farm equipment, locomotives, and tea-gathering machines for the local tea industry.

ENERGY

Georgia's mountainous territory has many fast-flowing rivers that provide a source of abundant energy. More than two hundred hydroelectric dams have been built to tap the energy of the Rioni, Kura, and Inguri Rivers. These plants supply most of the country's energy needs.

However, for natural gas and oil products, Georgia has to rely almost entirely on imports. Natural gas is imported mainly from Azerbaijan now, instead of from Russia, as in the past. The country produces 799.5 oil barrels (bbl) per day (one bbl equals forty-two US gallons, or 159 liters) and has a reserve of 35 million bbl. The constructions on the Baku—Tbilisi—Ceyhan oil pipeline and the Baku—Tbilisi—Erzerum gas pipeline have brought much-needed investment and job opportunities to Georgia. Construction of these pipelines, along with the South Caucasus gas pipeline, and the Kars-Akhalkalaki railroad, are part of an economic strategy to profit from Georgia's strategic location between Europe and Asia. The country hopes to develop its role as a transit point for gas, oil, and other goods. The expansion of the South Caucasus pipeline, which is part of the Shah Deniz II Southern

Gas Corridor project, is expected to bring $2 billion in foreign investment into the country. Gas from this project should begin flowing in 2019.

The northwest mountains yield coal, reserves of which are estimated to be about 400 million tons (360 million metric tons). Under Soviet rule these deposits were not mined, because other forms of fuel could be obtained cheaply elsewhere. Exploiting its natural resources to reduce reliance on outside suppliers is one of Georgia's most important goals.

TRANSPORTATION

Georgia has 11,874 miles (19,109 km) of roads and 847miles (1,363 km) of rail lines.

Three major roads cross the Great Caucasus to provide a link with Russia— the Georgian Military Highway links Tbilisi to Vladikavkaz, another highway links Kutaisi to Vladikavkaz, and the third one links Sukhumi to Cherkessk. Armenia, Azerbaijan, and Turkey are linked to Georgia by numerous roads.

Infrastructure has a crucial role to play in the economic development of the region. The country's roads and ports can provide a bridge for goods and services from the West via Turkey and the Black Sea to the new markets of the Caucasus and Asia. The ports of Batumi, Sukhumi, and Poti were busy import centers in the Soviet period, and may regain their influence as the region develops.

In 2006 Russia severed all air, sea, land, and railroad links with Georgia, as well as postal service and visa issuance because of a spy scandal. The only legal land border crossing at Zemo Larsi was also closed, diverting traffic into the separatist regions outside of Georgia's control. These harsh measures have led Georgia to seek new markets for their products elsewhere.

TOURISM

Georgia's tourism industry is growing rapidly, promoted by the Georgian National Tourism Administration (GNTA). This organization was founded in 2010 to develop a sustainable tourism industry by presenting Georgia as a unique travel destination on the international tourist map. In 2016, the number of international tourist arrivals reached a high of 2,714,773 and brought in about $2 billion in revenue. This is a great improvement over 1996, when only 600 foreign tourists visited Georgia. Most tourists come from the neighboring regions, as might be expected, with Azerbaijanis leading the way in 2016, closely followed by Armenians and Turks.

The small country has many attractions, including historical, religious, cultural, natural, and recreational destinations. Batumi in Ajaria has Black Sea beaches and there is skiing in the mountain regions. For history buffs, there are three UNESCO World Heritage Sites.

Borjomi, Georgia, is a resort town famous for its mineral water springs.

INTERNET LINKS

http://atlas.media.mit.edu/en/profile/country/geo
This site presents an overview of Georgia's economy using graphics.

https://www.lonelyplanet.com/georgia
Lonely Planet offers a look at Georgia's tourist attractions.

http://www.slate.com/articles/news_and_politics/roads/2016/12/ the_vanishing_svan_culture_fights_for_survival_in_northeast_ georgia.html
This article explains the Svan people's hope for greater tourism to their remote region.

ENVIRONMENT

Morning sunlight illuminates the foothills of Mount Shkhara, the highest peak in Georgia.

5

LIKE OTHER FORMER SOVIET republics, Georgia suffers from the long-term destructive environmental practices of that era. Since independence, and with the awakening of green awareness globally, Georgia has taken steps to evaluate and tackle its problems, including land degradation, deforestation, air pollution, and waste issues.

In 2016, the World Health Organization published research stating that air pollution caused an estimated 6.5 million deaths, or 11.6 percent of all global deaths in 2012, making it the largest single environmental health risk. It found Georgia to have the world's highest mortality rate linked to air pollution, with nearly 300 deaths per 100,000 due to air pollution.

A peacock at the Tbilisi Zoo, which is rebuilding after devastating floods in 2015 left hundreds of animals dead.

The medieval
stone-arched
Queen Tamar's
Bridge spans the
River Besletka
in Abkhazia.

LAND DEGRADATION AND DEFORESTATION

Erosion and a decline in land productivity are serious issues. Some 35 percent of the country's farmland is degraded as a result of poor land management practices—such as cattle overgrazing, unregulated waste disposal, and short-sighted agricultural activities; industrialization; and an increase in natural disasters such as flash floods and landslides. These extreme weather events are, in turn, the product of poor environmental stewardship and climate change, so it's a circular pattern of cause and effect.

Nearly 40 percent of Georgia is forested, and almost 10 percent of these forests are virgin old growth. Illegal and unregulated logging has been a major problem, exacerbated by rural poverty. The United Nations Economic Commission for Europe states that nearly 60 percent of the annual forest harvest is unrecorded fuel wood—poor people will readily resort to the illegal cutting of forests to supplement scarce fuel resources.

Georgia's forests and wildlife have suffered as a result. Such economic pressures have resulted in a significant reduction of endemic plant communities. Some are now rare or endangered, and a few have become extinct. These include the Georgian elm, the Transcaucasian poplar, and the Eldari pine. With deforestation some of the signature animals of the Caucasus regions have gone extinct or nearly so. Among these are the four species of wild goat, the Persian gazelle, the striped hyena, and the Caucasian leopard.

WATER POLLUTION

Industrial development during the Soviet era contributed to the pollution of the Black Sea.

There is now a heightened awareness of the pollution and ecological decline of the Black Sea, not only by the nations that surround it, like Georgia, but also by the European countries spanning or bordering the Danube River, which empties into it. Industrial, agricultural, and medical discharges continue to pollute the seas. Inadequate sewage treatment adds to the problem, as less than 20 percent of wastewater is treated before being released into the sea.

These hazards also affect water systems throughout Georgia. In addition power shortages often prevent the effective delivery of drinking water to the population. An estimated 70 percent of surface water in Georgia contains health-endangering bacteria. This may account for Georgia's high rate of intestinal disease.

Plastic bottles and other garbage contaminate a river in Georgia.

AIR POLLUTION

Road traffic is the major source of air pollution in Georgia, followed by the energy sector and industry. Until the year 2000, Georgia used leaded fuel in most of their vehicles, which led to high concentrations of lead and benzene in the air.

Numerous hazardous sources of ionizing radiation, such as communications equipment containing radioactive strontium and cesium, have been discovered in areas formerly occupied by Russian forces. In 1986 a nuclear power plant exploded in Chernobyl, some 750 miles (1200 km) away, in Ukraine. Prevailing winds brought radiation across the Black Sea. Georgia has since documented an increase of up to 20 percent more cases of anemia, a condition in which there is a deficiency of red cells or hemoglobin in the blood, resulting in pallor and weariness, in pregnant women. Primary endocrine system diseases, as well as cancer and related sicknesses, have also increased since the accident.

In the post-Soviet years the Georgian government attributed little importance to the country's environmental problems. In 1993 the minister for protection of the environment resigned in protest of this inactivity. In January 1994 a new, interdepartmental environmental monitoring system was introduced by the Cabinet of Ministers to centralize separate programs under the direction of the Ministry of Protection of the Environment. The Green Party fought vigorously on environmental issues in the parliament in 1993.

INTERNET LINKS

http://www.blackseascene.net
This organization provides information on the environmental issues facing the Black Sea.

http://www.georgianjournal.ge/society/32635-georgia-no-1-among-the-countries-that-have-deadliest-air-pollution.html
This article looks at Georgia's serious air pollution problem.

http://documents.worldbank.org/curated/en/293731468001755898/pdf/ACS13945-WP-P147475-Box391501B-PUBLIC-6-26-15.pdf
This 2015 World Bank report provides a thorough examination of environmental challenges in Georgia.

GEORGIANS

A young woman dances wearing traditional Georgian clothing.

6

FOR SUCH A SMALL COUNTRY, modern Georgia is certainly an ethnically diverse place. Many Georgians trace their ancestry to traders, invaders, and refugees from neighboring lands who settled in Georgia over the centuries. Because the country is mountainous, its people are divided into many small, independent groups.

In a mountain village, traditionally dressed people perform folk tunes.

The Friendship Arch in Kazbegi is a famous landmark along the Georgian Military Highway in the Caucasus Mountains.

A 1989 Soviet census listed ninety-six distinct nationalities in Georgia. During that era, the goal was to gradually merge the many nationalities of the Soviet Union into the "Soviet person"—one that would practice socialist principles and put political ideology before national culture. But the peoples of Georgia managed to hold on to their national spirit, despite pressure from Moscow.

That national spirit, however, broke apart as well, into smaller ethnic and regional allegiances. Just trying to discuss "the people of Georgia" brings up the slippery question of what is, or is not, Georgia—and who is, or is not, Georgian.

Although the government of Georgia considers Abkhazia and South Ossetia to be part of Georgia, it did not count the people in those regions for its 2014 census. Why? Because those regions were not under government control at the time and it was literally unable to count them. That holds true at this writing, in 2017, as well.

Therefore, not counting the people of Abkhazia and South Ossetia, there are about 3.7 million people in the country. (Including them would bring the total population of the country to about 4.9 million.) Of those, ethnic Georgians make up 86.8 percent, or 3.2 million people. The other major ethnic groups are the Azeri (or Azerbaijanis) at 6.3 percent; and Armenians at 4.5 percent. People of other ethnicities, including Russians, Ossetians, Yazidis, Ukrainians, Kists, and Greeks, constitute a mere 2.3 percent.

However, there's a catch. Since the Abkhazia and South Ossetia provinces were not counted in this census, the percentages of Abkhazians, at 0.2 percent, and Ossetians, at 0.4 percent, are much lower than they would be if the entire country was counted. Likewise, the percentage of ethnic Georgians skews much higher than it otherwise would be.

KARTVELIAN PEOPLES

Georgians distinguish three Kartvelian peoples—the Georgians, Mingrelians, and Svans. A fourth group, called Laz, lives almost exclusively in modern-day Turkey. The Kartvelian people share a common language, history, and culture. The origin of the Kartvelians as a people is not known, but they are probably the result of a fusion of aboriginal Caucasian peoples with immigrants from Asia Minor. Nowadays, when people refer to Georgians, they usually mean all Kartvelian peoples, including the Svans and Mingrelians.

GEORGIANS   The Georgians call themselves *Kartvelebi* (kart-VE-le-bi) and their country *Sakartvelo* (sa-KART-ve-lo). These names are linked to the mythical demigod Kartlos (said to be a great-great-grandson of Moses), who is considered the "father" of all Georgians. Some historians believe the country's English name comes from its patron saint, Saint George. But the most likely theory is that the name "Georgia" originates from "Gurj," the name given to the people of Georgia by the Arabs and Persians.

Physically Georgians resemble the peoples of the eastern Mediterranean, but they are generally taller, with athletic, wiry bodies and dark hair and eyes. The Georgians are proud, passionate, and fiercely individualistic, retaining a strong sense of family. They are renowned fighters with strict codes of personal honor and a long tradition of chivalry. They are hospitable, welcoming guests and travelers. Friendship is highly prized and celebrated in the country's twelfth-century national epic, *The Knight in the Panther's Skin*, written by Shota Rustaveli, the great medieval Georgian poet.

The people behave and carry themselves with dignity and what many observers consider a sense of royalty. According to an unofficial census conducted many years ago, as many as one in seven Georgians claimed to be of royal descent.

MINGRELIANS Nearly one million Mingrelians, a subgroup of Georgians, live in the country; the majority in the region of Samegrelo, their traditional homeland in the western part of Georgia that borders the Black Sea. It also lies adjacent to the breakaway region of Abkazia, and many Mingrelians find themselves caught up in the political tensions there. Unlike other Georgians, these people tend to have fair skin, blond hair, and blue eyes, which are rarities in this part of the world.

SVANS There are approximately thirty thousand Svans in Georgia who live mainly in the mountainous regions of Upper and Lower Svaneti. Throughout the Middle Ages, the Mongol invasions, and the Turkish and Persian incursions of the sixteenth and seventeenth centuries, the Svans found themselves cut off from the mainstream of Georgian cultural and social life, safe and isolated in their mountain fortresses. Consequently their dialect has much in common with older rather than modern forms of Georgian.

The character of the Svans is very much a product of their harsh, mountainous environment. They are a proud, independent, and hardy people used to a stoical existence with few of the comforts of modern civilization. Hunters and climbers are the most respected members of the community. Vendettas and blood feuds between communities and families continue to this day. However, the Svans, like all Georgians, are very hospitable toward guests and travelers. They are famous for their songs, which are a complex form of Georgian polyphonic singing, and their dances.

AJARANS The people of the Ajarian Autonomous Republic are mainly ethnic Georgians, although the majority is made up of Muslims. This is a result of

Ottoman Turkish rule from the sixteenth to nineteenth centuries. Many Ajarians still have close cultural and family ties with the bordering Turkish provinces.

ABKHAZIANS

There are approximately 122,000 Abkhazians in Georgia. Despite their small numbers, they are a visible minority because they inhabit their own republic, the Abkhazian Autonomous Republic, along the northwest coast of the Black Sea.

The origin of the Abkhazian people is shrouded in mystery, although they have been in Georgia for about two thousand years. They are thought to be a proto-Georgian people who, in the seventeenth century, mixed with the Adige, a northern Caucasian tribe, and, in doing so, lost their Georgian-oriented culture.

The Abkhazians are ethnically a northern Caucasian people who are different from the Kartvelian, or southern Caucasian people. They are a mountain people who have traditionally lived as shepherds.

The people have their own government and language, Abkhaz. Russian is spoken as a second language. Few Abkhazians speak good Georgian, although many of those who live in the south of Abkhazia, near Samegrelo, speak Mingrelian, the dialect of that region. About half of Abkhazians are Orthodox Christians and half are Sunni Muslims.

People enjoy the day at a town park in Gagra, in Abkhazia.

OSSETIANS

The 2014 census puts the population of Ossetians in Georgia (excluding South Ossetia itself) at 14,500. About 529,000 are in Russia. Only 45,000 live in South Ossetia. The Ossetians are an Iranian people and are thought to be descendants of the ancient Alans, who came to the region in the sixth century CE. They are essentially a mountain people and most of them are Christians, though there is a sizable Muslim minority, differences that set them apart from the Georgians. Many Ossetians want to withdraw from the Georgian republic and unite their region with North Ossetia, which lies in Russia. The Georgians, however, believe that South Ossetia is historically a part of Inner Kartli and so they have resisted the separation.

OTHER PEOPLES

Because of the constant movement of people and shifts of power throughout the history of the Caucasus, many other peoples from the surrounding region have settled in Georgia. There are also about 233,000 Azerbaijanis in Georgia, the majority of whom live south of Tbilisi, in and around the towns of Bolnisi and Marneuli. Most speak Azerbaijani and are Muslims.

There are some 168,000 Armenians in the country. The Armenians are Christians and have their own language and alphabet. They are spread throughout the world, mainly because of historical persecution by the dominant Turkish and Arab Muslims in what was once West Armenia. Tbilisi has a large Armenian population, as do the regions of Meskheti and Dzhavakheti.

About 26,600 ethnic Russians live in Georgia, about 6,000 Ukrainians, 5,700 Caucasus Greeks, and even smaller numbers of Kurds, Assyrian, Jews, and miscellaneous others.

DRESS

Occasionally on festival days, during celebrations, or for the fun of it, the Georgians dress in their distinctive traditional costume. Men wear the

South Ossetians read Russian newspapers in the region's capital, Tskhinvali.

cherkeska (CHER-kes-kah), a knee-length tunic worn with soft, high, leather boots, and a *burkah* (BUR-kah), or woolen cape, flung over their shoulders. Georgian men like to appear masculine, and often wear daggers for special occasions, as well as cartridge cases sewn on the chest of their *chokhas*, or tunics.

In Svaneti and Kakheti cylindrical-shaped woolen caps are traditional. The women also wear cherkeskas, although theirs are usually longer than the men's and are decorated with etched silver chains and buckles. Many women in the rural areas wear headscarves, but this traditional headgear is losing its popularity in cities.

INTERNET LINKS

https://www.discoverabkhazia.org/abkhazia
This site introduces the region of Abkhazia including a discussion of its people and traditional clothing.

http://expnowhere.com/culture/ossetian-peope-and-their-culture
This site offers a good overview of the Ossetian people.

http://factsanddetails.com/russia/Minorities/sub9_3d/ entry-5116.html
This overview of the Svan people gives information in bullet points.

http://ngm.nationalgeographic.com/2014/10/svanetia/larmer-text
This article provides a good look at the Svaneti region and its people.

http://www.vogue.com/article/georgia-traditional-chokha- fashion-trend
This *Vogue* article asserts that the chokha is an international fashion trend

LIFESTYLE

A farmer carries dried corn stalks on a horse-drawn cart in the village of Atskhuri, Georgia in 2016.

7

GEORGIANS REGARD THE mountainous provinces of the Caucasus to be the heart and soul of their country. Many of their traditions are thought to have originated there—the lavish hospitality, sense of honor, and the importance placed on friendship.

Hospitality, generosity, and friendship are the codes by which Georgians live. They are known for their uninhibited hospitality, accosting friends and even strangers regularly and inviting them into their homes for an impromptu drink, snack, or meal. Georgian hospitality often means that meals last for hours and consist of many courses, toasts, and lengthy arguments and discussions.

The mountainous areas are thinly populated compared with the lowlands. The lifestyle there is pastoral and lacks the advantages of modern technology. People generally make their living as shepherds and by growing a few vegetables on the limited amount of fertile land. The weather is harsh during the winter months, and there are frequent landslides and road accidents. Along many mountain roads, it is common to find small, cagelike structures that serve as memorials that mark the spot where someone was killed. Inside each memorial is a picture of the deceased, a bottle of wine, and some drinking glasses. This allows passing friends and relatives to stop and drink to the memory of their loved one.

According to Georgian etiquette, both men and women may kiss one another on the cheek in public places. However, more intimate gestures, even between spouses, are frowned upon in public. In the countryside, it is polite to greet strangers. Shaking hands is common, but women tend to shake hands less often than men do.

New apartment buildings in Batumi boast whimsical modern architectural design.

COUNTRY AND CITY LIFE

Life in the cities improved during the Soviet era, but mountain communities were generally left out of the technological advances made in the lowland areas. This led to a steady drift of people to the cities.

In the cities it is popular to take a walk after work. People are in the habit of strolling up and down the main thoroughfares in the evening, talking, laughing, and occasionally going into a café for a glass of wine, brandy, or coffee. This custom offers young Georgians the opportunity to meet one another. In Tbilisi the most popular place for taking an evening walk is the tree-lined Rustaveli Avenue. Around this street are Tbilisi's best cafés, restaurants, shops, cinemas, and theaters. Elsewhere there is always something going on—people buying and selling things, playing games or musical instruments, eating together, or just chatting.

In the villages most people work on the land. It is common for Georgians to have their own fruit or vegetable plots and, in some cases, even vineyards in their back garden. The people's lives are dominated by the changing

The Georgians love to celebrate, and they take great pride in their toasting. Toasts are always initiated by the tamada (TA-ma-da), or toastmaster. Once the tamada has proposed the toast and drunk, the other guests may follow. If a toast honors a particular person, the assembled guests drink to that person first, allowing the individual to respond with a final toast of thanks.

Often a special or honored guest will be presented with a khantsi (KAN-tsi), a large goat's horn filled to the brim with wine, and asked to drain it all at once. Important toasts usually mean that the glass is drained in a single gulp as a sign of respect. The last toast will be in honor of the tamada, and to a safe journey home. As the Georgians would say, "Gauma ... jos!" (ga-u-MA ... jos), or "Cheers!"

seasons. For example, Kakheti is a hive of activity in October when grapes are harvested. The villagers celebrate the bounty by decorating the balconies of their houses with bunches of grapes, and every available basket and bucket is filled to the brim with grapes.

Although Georgians love their wine, they consider it in bad taste to get drunk. The measure of a man's masculinity is often equated with his ability to hold his drink.

MALE DOMINATION

Georgia is a male-oriented society where the birth of a baby boy is celebrated more than that of a girl. Boys are usually spoiled by their mothers, which contributes to their sense of superiority. Georgian male role models are traditional and often old-fashioned. The most admired men in Georgia are bandits, warriors, and horsemen from the country's eventful past, all of whom are remembered in popular songs and dances. Boys are often named after these popular figures. Such role models influence the men's attitudes and reinforce the image of the macho male. This image is further reflected in the traditional costumes worn by men on special occasions—they are usually decked out in cherkeska and carry a sword, dagger, and gun cartridges.

Male and female roles are very clearly defined, and gender equality is not an issue in Georgia as it is in Western countries. Although they are not an inhibited people, the Georgians do observe a strict code of sexual morality. The men treat women with great respect, but not necessarily as equals. For example, the men are unlikely to help with household chores such as washing or cooking, which they consider feminine tasks.

Georgian women are traditionally feminine in their behavior and are not likely to engage in masculine work or pastimes. In the cities, more women are financially independent, but are likely to live with their families until they marry, as is the case with their male counterparts.

FAMILY AND MARRIAGE

Georgians are traditional in their ways, and family and marriage form the cornerstone of society. Traditionally, the man's family seeks a bride and initiates marriage negotiations. This is normally done through a female relative, who assesses the suitability of unmarried women in the locality. A "chance" meeting will then be arranged to give the man and woman an opportunity to see one another. If there is some attraction, they will meet again, after which the man or a member of his family will approach the woman's parents to ask for her hand in marriage. When the marriage proposal is accepted, the groom produces a gold ring to mark the engagement. The bride's family gives a dowry, although this is usually small.

Church wedding ceremonies were rare during the Soviet era, but the tradition was gradually revived with the demise of communism and an increase in religious practice. The main wedding ceremony is a social rather than a religious event. First the groom goes to the bride's house in a ribbon-decked car, followed by a noisy, colorful convoy of his family members. Following this the couple goes to a registry office to register the marriage and exchange rings. A celebration at the groom's home follows, with dinner, toasts, singing, and dancing, attended by the couple's families.

A *tamada*, usually one of the groom's uncles, acts as master of ceremonies. That night the couple

A bride poses with her family in front of Sioni Cathedral in Tbilisi.

spends their first night together in their own bedroom in the groom's family house. Feasting usually continues for several days. The day after the wedding, the bride is traditionally taken to fetch water from the local spring, where she will have the opportunity to meet the womenfolk of her new neighborhood.

In the past, rural Georgians generally married someone from their home area, often from the same village. As a result of the increased social mobility that came with being a part of the Soviet Union, marriages among people from different parts of Georgia and even across the Soviet Union became more common.

EDUCATION

Education has always been important to Georgians, and centers of learning can be traced back as far as the time of the Colchians. For much of history the Georgian Church ran the schools, providing the country with an educated class.

Education is mandatory for all children from the age of six to fourteen. The school system is divided into elementary (six years; ages six to twelve), basic (three years; ages twelve to fifteen), and secondary (three years; ages

CENTENARIANS

Georgians—particularly the people of Abkhazia (the breakaway republic no longer considers itself a part of Georgia)—are famous for their longevity. In 1977, a Dannon TV commercial aired in the United States that featured elderly rural Abkhazians—then living in Soviet Georgia—claiming to be well over 100 years old. Their secret, the ad implied, was a lifetime of eating yogurt. Even today, numerous Georgian and Abkhaz sources claim elders of 130 years old or more. The republic has claimed 51 centenarians—people who have lived 100 years or more—for every 100,000 inhabitants.

However, the Georgian claims have not stood up to scrutiny. The problem is one of dubious recordkeeping. So far, according to verifiable documentation, the world's longest-living person was Jeanne Louise Calment (1875–1997) of France, who lived to be 122. And the country with the largest percentage of centenarians, by far, is Japan with 48 oldsters per 100,000 people. Many areas of the world simply don't have any reliable documentation from a century or more ago, and Georgia—in fact, all of the former Soviet Union—appears to fall into that category.

Meanwhile, today, the average life expectancy at birth for men in Georgia is 72.1 years, and for women, 80.6 years—unremarkable figures compared with those of the rest of the world.

While claims of extreme old age have been around since biblical times, most accounts have to be regarded as legend. A list of all the verified *supercentenarians—humans who have lived to at least 110—in all of history adds up to merely 1,700-plus people as of 2015. And not one of those was from Georgia.*

Naturally, this doesn't mean Georgia—or Abkhazia—does not, in fact, have a robust population of very old people. It simply means their reputation for oldsters has been earned anecdotally, rather than factually. The Georgian centenarians don't just live a long time; they reportedly live full lives, working, relaxing, and enjoying themselves as they always have. Abkhazia boasts a famous choir called Nartaa (NAR-ta) made up wholly of men seventy to one hundred years old and older.

Is yogurt, in fact, the secret? Diet may very well be a contributing factor in long life, gerontology research experts say, along with genetic heritage, lifestyle, and any number of other things. The truth is, nobody knows for sure—at least not yet.

fifteen to eighteen). Alternatively, secondary students can choose two years of vocational studies.

Under the Soviet system, all Georgians were guaranteed free preschool, primary, secondary, and higher education. As a result, Georgia has one of the highest proportions of college graduates among former Soviet countries.

On the other hand, the country has a reputation for corruption in higher education. An old Soviet joke explains the tradition of bribery: A man visits a college professor and says, "My son has an exam with you tomorrow, but he is not well prepared. I am afraid that he will fail." Without raising his head, the professor replies, "I bet you $500 your son will pass."

Officials estimate some $30 million were spent on bribes every year, more than the country's entire education budget. This was possible because each university administered and graded its own entrance exams. In an effort to quash the corrupt system, in 2005, Georgian Education Minister Alexander Lomaia instituted a state-administered test. Only the students who have passed the Unified National Examinations may now enroll in a state-accredited institution of higher education. Lomaia also established other reforms. The curriculum was modernized and Westernized, and many professors were replaced. The changes did not make Lomaia popular with his fellow Georgians, but did improve the overall education of Georgian students.

There are twenty-four state colleges and universities in Georgia, as well as eighty-one accredited private institutions. There is a medical school, an art academy, a music conservatory, and a theater institute—all in Tbilisi. The Ivane Javakhishvili Tbilisi State University, or TSU, is Georgia's largest institution of higher learning. It was founded in 1917, following the Russian Revolution. It offers bachelors, masters, and doctoral degree programs in a wide variety of subjects and has five branches throughout the country. About twenty-two thousand students attend the university.

HEALTH CARE

All Georgians are entitled to basic health care. Georgia's state-financed healthcare system provides universal care for about 90 percent of the population. However, Georgia's government has struggled to find the funds

As late as the year 2000, homosexuality was against the law in Georgia. Parliament decriminalized it at the beginning of the new millennium, not, many people suspect, because of a change in social attitudes, but as an appeasement to Europe and the rest of the West. In 2014, the Georgian parliament went further and banned discrimination on the basis of sexual orientation and gender identity.

Nevertheless, public attitudes have largely not caught up with the law. Homosexuality is widely considered to be deviant behavior, with some surveys showing more than 90 percent of Georgians finding it to be "completely unacceptable." Same-sex marriage is not legal and some people want to amend the constitution to ban it permanently.

The leading critic of any acquiescence to LGBT rights is the head of the Georgian Orthodox Church, Patriarch Ilia II. Born in 1933, he has been the head of the church since 1977. His opinion carries an enormous amount of weight in the country, where, in 2010, a CNN poll found him to be "the most trusted man in Georgia." In 2013, Ilia II described homosexuality as a disease and compared it to drug addiction. While he hasn't advocated violence against gay people or rights proponents, homophobic attacks are not uncommon in Georgia and tend to escape punishment.

to support the program. Most hospitals and clinics were privatized after independence, and health insurance was handled by private insurance companies. The result left a large portion of people unable to afford health insurance, and after the 2012 elections, Georgia's new ruling coalition looked to expand state-funded care.

The Georgian Dream party implemented universal healthcare between 2013 and 2014, along with other related reforms. However, although the state spends 2 percent of its GDP on healthcare, which is only about half what many European countries spend, it is still coming up short. Improving efficiency and containing costs appear to be two goals that are now being pursued to solve the problem.

INTERNET LINKS

http://www.everyculture.com/wc/Costa-Rica-to-Georgia/Georgians.html
This look at the culture of Georgia provides general information about lifestyle.

http://georgiatoday.ge/news/3402/Georgia%E2%80%99s-Healthcare-Reform
This article provides a good overview of Georgia's healthcare reforms.

http://www.mes.gov.ge/?lang=eng
Georgia's Ministry of Education and Science offers some up-to-date news stories in English.

https://muftah.org/hate-crime-acquittal-highlights-institutionalized-homophobia-in-georgia/#.WRsmA2grLcs
This 2015 article focuses on the state of LGBT rights in Georgia.

https://www.tsu.ge/en
This is the English-language website of the Ivane Javakhishvili Tbilisi State University.

RELIGION

A recently restored medieval monastery church sits atop the Katskhi pillar, a natural limestone monolith, in

8

GEORGIA IS A PREDOMINANTLY orthodox christian country. Although there is no official state religion, the Georgian Orthodox Church, a branch of Eastern Orthodoxy, is accorded special importance and is nominally supported by 82.3 percent of the population. Throughout history, and especially during the tsarist and Soviet eras, the Georgian Orthodox Church provided a powerful focus for the country's patriotism and nationalism. Today it is the most trusted institution in Georgia.

However, Georgia is also a diverse country where freedom of religious expression is guaranteed in the constitution. In Tbilisi, for example, there is a Jewish synagogue, a Muslim mosque, a Georgian basilica, an Armenian church, and a Zoroastrian temple, all within a 15-minute walk of one another.

According to the 2014 census, the other main religions in the republic are Islam (10.7 percent), the Armenian Apostolic Church (2.9 percent), the Russian Orthodox Church (1 percent), and the Roman Catholic Church (0.5–1 percent). Another 2 percent belong to other religions or no religion.

The unusual shape of the Georgian cross, with its slightly drooping horizontal arms, is ascribed to Saint Nino. The legend says that upon entering Georgia, she took two vine branches and tied them into a cross using strands from her own hair, thus making an imperfect cross. As the symbol of the Georgian Orthodox Church, it's also known as the "grapevine cross" or "Saint Nino's cross."

The majestic interior of the medieval Gelati Monastery, founded in 1106, is a masterpiece of Georgia's Golden Age.

GEORGIAN ORTHODOX CHURCH

Christianity came to Georgia in 330 CE. The story of the country's conversion is a mixture of fact and legend. Tradition says that a slave woman, who later came to be known as Saint Nino, cured the Iberian Queen Nana of a strange illness. This proved Nino's holiness and helped her gain the queen's confidence. Legend has it that the queen's husband, King Mirian, was converted when he found himself enveloped suddenly in pitch darkness while on a hunting trip. He then invoked the Christian God, and the light of day returned. It is thought that he actually saw an eclipse of the sun and mistook it for a divine event.

In western Georgia, Christianity replaced early beliefs that were based on a pantheon of Greek gods, and in eastern Georgia it replaced an Iranian Zoroastrian religion. The conversion to Christianity had a profound effect on Georgian culture and history. The country suddenly became one of the few Eastern outposts of Christianity with its cultural and social orientation toward Christian Europe, away from the Islamic civilizations to the south and east.

In the fifth century, the church became autonomous and appointed its own leader, the Catholicos of Mtskheta. Throughout the Middle Ages the Georgian Church held enormous political and economic power and inspired a tradition of art, architecture, and literature.

Under tsarist rule, however, the church lost its independence and was treated as a branch of its much larger brother, the Russian Orthodox Church. The independent status of the Georgian Church was reestablished during the Soviet era when Joseph Stalin—who had trained for the priesthood in Georgia—intervened on its behalf. Despite this, many of the two thousand churches in Georgia were closed and left to deteriorate, and it is only over the last thirty years that the churches have been reopened and restoration work has begun.

PRACTICES The Georgian Orthodox Church is part of the Eastern branch of Christianity, the Orthodox Church. It is practiced in much of Eastern Europe and Greece. The Eastern churches split formally from Western Christianity in the eleventh century, and do not recognize the Pope in Rome as their head, nor do they observe any of the Western Church's holy days. The Orthodox churches have never had a central body or leader, as the Catholic Church does. The current head of the Georgian Church is Catholicos Ilia II (b. 1933). Georgian Orthodox practice is similar to that of the other Orthodox churches, although it differs in some of its liturgical rules and rituals. Christmas and Easter are the most important days in the Georgian Orthodox calendar.

Orthodox practice has more in common with Catholic rather than Protestant practice. Ritual is important and includes music, the burning of incense, and chanting. Icons are positioned around the inside of most churches, and walls are covered with frescoes depicting religious events. Believers pray in front of the icons, lighting candles as offerings and often kissing the icons as a mark of devotion. Orthodox services are usually sung in Georgian. The combined experience is intended to convey the essence of Christianity, appealing to worshippers' emotional, intellectual, and aesthetic faculties.

Since the late 1980s there has been a revival of faith in Georgia, especially among the rural population. More children are being baptized, and church weddings are becoming popular. The government has encouraged the revival as a healthy expression of the national spirit.

RUSSIAN ORTHODOX CHURCH

Christianity reached Georgia before it reached Russia; the Georgian Orthodox Church is older than the much larger Russian Orthodox Church by about six centuries.

In Georgia only 1 percent of the people are Russian Orthodox Christians. Russian Orthodoxy originated in Kievan Rus (the kingdom of Rus, originally

Saint George is the patron saint of Georgia (and also of England, Portugal, Romania, and myriad cities, towns, and provinces across the Christian world). The facts of his historical life are uncertain but according to legends, he might have been a Roman soldier of Greek origin who lived from 280 to 303 CE.

The most famous myth associated with the saint, his slaying of a dragon, is a tale that arose during the times of the Crusades. Icons showing George slaying a dragon are often found in Georgian churches. In pagan times, the worship of heroes and warriors was common. Saint George, as a strong and dashing warrior saint, was the ideal figure to fill this role after the country's conversion to Christianity, and he is revered even today.

In Georgia, particularly in rural areas, there are many folk tales about the venerated saint. According to one myth, Saint George was cut into 365 pieces after he fell in battle and every piece was spread throughout the country. Another myth claims that Saint George appeared in person during the Battle of Didgori in 1121 to help King David IV ("the Builder") defeat the much larger invading Seljuq Turkish army. The "miraculous victory" freed Georgia from Persian rule. Saint George is therefore considered by many Georgians to have special meaning as a symbol of national liberation.

in the region of Kiev, Ukraine) in the tenth century when Christianity first arrived there. Over the next few centuries it became the religion of all Russians. In the nineteenth century Russian and Ukrainian migrants brought it to Georgia from tsarist Russia. The tsarist authorities encouraged the establishment of monasteries in an attempt to strengthen their influence in the region as part of their Russification policy. One of the most famous of these is Novy Afon (New Athos), built in Abkhazia in 1900. Russian churches are found mainly along the coast of the Black Sea and in larger cities such as Tbilisi and Kutaisi.

The Russian Orthodox Church is the world's largest Eastern Orthodox church and is the chief representative of the precepts of Orthodoxy. The head of the church is the Patriarch of All Russia.

ARMENIAN APOSTOLIC CHURCH

The Armenian Apostolic Church is marginally older than the Georgian Orthodox Church, and was founded in the late third century by Gregory the Illuminator. In converting the Armenian king (King Tiridates III), Gregory, in effect, created the world's first truly Christian state. The Armenian Church separated from the other Eastern churches in the sixth century and is still autonomous today. It is headed by the Catholicos of Echmiadzin near Yerevan, Armenia.

Armenian churches tend to have simple decorations. They practice the custom of hanging ostrich eggs from the ceilings of the churches as symbols of hope and resurrection. Georgia contains the largest community of practicing Apostolic Armenians outside of Armenia. Armenians first began migrating to Georgia in the fourteenth and fifteenth centuries as a result of persecution by the Muslim Turks and Arabs.

ISLAM

Islam is a major religion in the Caucasus—many of the peoples in the Russian regions north of Georgia are Muslim, as are the populations of Turkey and Azerbaijan. Georgia has historically been perched on the northern edge of

Mtskheta is one of the oldest cities in Georgia, dating to the fifth century BCE. Located about 12 miles (20 km) north of Tbilisi, it was the ancient capital of Kartli, the East Georgian Kingdom that existed from the third century BCE to the fifth century CE. It is also the location where Christianity was proclaimed as the official religion of Georgia in 337 CE. In 2014, the Georgian Orthodox Church declared it to be a "Holy City." Today, Mtskheta still remains the headquarters of the Georgian Orthodox and Apostolic Church.

Three medieval churches in the city together form a World Heritage Site that UNESCO has designated as the Historical Monuments of Mtskheta. The property consists of the Jvari Monastery, the Svetitstkhoveli Cathedral, and the Samtavro Monastery, and was added to the World Heritage List in 1994. According to the World Heritage Centre, the churches represent

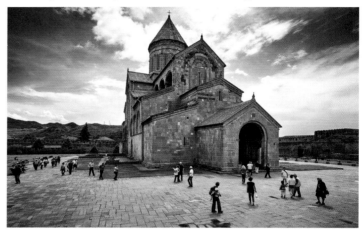

"outstanding examples of medieval religious architecture in the Caucasus" and "show the high artistic and cultural level attained by this ancient kingdom.

The Cathedral of Svetitskhoveli s one of the most sacred places in Georgia. The site was chosen for one of Georgia's first churches in the fourth century because it was the burial place of an early Georgian saint, Sidonia. A cedar tree grew from the grave, and King Mirian ordered seven columns to be made from its trunk to provide the church's foundations. It is said that when the sixth column was completed, the seventh rose magically by itself into the air and could only be put into place when Saint Nino interceded through prayer. It was also believed that a sacred liquid flowing from the column could cure all diseases. In Georgian the word sveti *(SVE-ti) means "column," and* tskhoveli *(ts-KOV-el-i) means "life-giving."*

the Islamic world, and the Islamic religion has left its mark on the republic. Georgia's Azerbaijani population consists of Azerbaijians, as well as the Abkhazians, Ossetians, and most of the ethnic Georgians in Ajaria.

JUDAISM

There have been Jewish communities in Georgia since the Middle Ages or even earlier. The largest Jewish communities are found in Kutaisi and Tbilisi; smaller groups can be found in the mountain regions. At one time 2 percent of the population of Kutaisi was Jewish, although over the last several decades, the Jewish presence has been reduced significantly by massive emigration to Israel in the 1990s. There are fewer than three thousand Jews in Georgia today.

INTERNET LINKS

https://georgianorthodoxchurch.wordpress.com
This lay site (not an official church site, since there isn't one available in English) offers information about the Georgian Church for English speakers.

http://www.haaretz.com/israel-news/videos/1.640351
This article, with photos and video, offers a good overview of Jewish history in Georgia.

http://www.newworldencyclopedia.org/entry/Saint_George
Information about the life, legends, and religious veneration of Saint George is found on this site.

http://whc.unesco.org/en/list/708
This is the UNESCO listing for the Historical Monuments of Mtskheta.

Even in the Georgian language, this sign is recognizable as an iconic McDonald's.

WITHIN THE SMALL AREA OF THE Caucasus there is an enormous variety of languages. Consequently many different languages are spoken in Georgia. The Roman writer Pliny recorded in the first century CE that the Romans needed 130 different interpreters to do business in the Caucasus. Strabo, the ancient Greek geographer, recorded in the same period that as many as seventy different languages were spoken daily in the market in Dioscuris (modern-day Sukhumi).

Georgian is the most widely spoken of the Caucasian languages. It is the official language of the Georgian republic and is spoken by approximately 87.6 percent of Georgia's population. Other local languages are spoken domestically in the various regions of the nation. And in the breakaway republic of Abkhazia, Abkhaz is the official language.

GEORGIAN

Georgian belongs to the Kartvelian (South Caucasian) family of languages, which also includes Mingrelian, Laz, and the archaic Svan. All of these languages originated from Old Kartvelian (circa 2000 BCE).

Like English, Georgian has no grammatical gender. That is, in English, nouns use the gender-neutral article *the*; whereas some languages, such as Spanish and French, for example, use gendered articles— *el* or *la* in Spanish; *le* or *la* in French. However, in Georgian—unlike in English—even the pronouns (*he* and *she*, for example) are gender-neutral.

The inscriptions can still be clearly seen on this ancient wall.

Georgian does not fit into any of the major European language groups.

Of the more than seventy Caucasian peoples—excluding the Armenians—only the Georgians had a written language of their own before Russian colonization in the nineteenth century. Because of Georgia's turbulent history, the Greco-Roman, Persian, Arabic, Turkish, and, most recently, Russian, languages have all left their mark on the Georgian language.

Russian was the only compulsory language taught in Georgian schools during the Soviet era. Following independence, however, learning Georgian has become compulsory for all Georgians, and all of the main curriculum subjects in schools are taught in Georgian.

REGIONAL DIALECTS The Georgian literary standard is based on the language of the Kartli region around the capital, Tbilisi. However, Georgian includes a number of regional dialects: Imeruli (spoken in Imereti), Rachuli (spoken in Racha), Guruli (spoken in Guria), Khaxuri (spoken in Kakheti), and Acharuli (spoken in Ajaria). Minor dialects such as Psavuri, Xevsuruli, Tusuri, and Mtiulur-Gudamaqruli are also spoken in the remote mountain regions of Pyavi, Khevsureti, Tusheti, and Mtiuleti, respectively.

HISTORY OF THE GEORGIAN LANGUAGE

The Georgian alphabet was originally developed to aid the spread of Christianity. Christianity became the official religion of Iberia (modern-day Kartli and Kakheti) and Armenia in the fourth century CE. The Iberians used Greek and Syriac texts for worship, but soon found a pressing need for a vernacular language to spread the new religion. A commission was set up to produce an alphabet that would represent the sounds of the Georgian and Armenian languages. In the fifth century a system of writing based on the

Greek alphabet was developed. The oldest Georgian inscriptions that have been discovered date from 430 CE and were found in a church near Bethlehem in Israel.

Georgian texts have traditionally been grouped into one of three periods: old Georgian (fifth to eleventh centuries), medieval Georgian (twelfth to eighteenth centuries), and modern Georgian (eighteenth century to the present). Medieval Georgian reached its zenith in the periods of David the Builder and Queen Tamar, especially in the work of Georgia's greatest lyrical poet, Shota Rustaveli.

Georgia only began to recover from the ravages of the Mongol conquest in the eighteenth century, and a unified literary language developed and flourished in the nineteenth century. Ilya Chavchavadze (1837—1907), the famous writer, did the most to modernize and promote the developing Georgian literary language. During the same period Jacob Gogebashvili (1840—1912) wrote *The Georgian Alphabet* (1865) and the definitive book on the Georgian language, *Native Speech* (1876).

Under the Soviet system Georgian was recognized as a state language of one of the Soviet Union's constituent republics and was consequently allowed to flourish with institutional support.

THE GEORGIAN ALPHABET

Since its adaptation into a written form, the Georgian language has progressed through three alphabet systems. The one used today is called *Mkhedruli* (m-ked-RU-li), meaning "secular writing." It is so called because in the eleventh century it replaced a script called "church writing." The spelling for Mkhedruli script is straightforward: Each letter has its own pronunciation, and each sound always corresponds to the same letter. There are no long vowel sounds in Georgian.

There are thirty-three letters in the modern Georgian alphabet, including five vowels and twenty-eight consonants. Several additional letters are

The Deda Ena statue in Tbilisi commemorates April 14, 1978, the day the Georgian people protested the Soviet decision to eliminate Georgian as an official state language and replace it with Russian. After the mass demonstration, Moscow backed down.

A sign in a bakery in Batumi says, "Fresh bread for sale."

now considered obsolete, but show up in other related alphabets, such as Mingrelian, Laz, and Svan. There is no distinction between upper- and lowercase letters. Like most languages, Georgian is written from left to right.

LEARNING GEORGIAN

Georgian (also known as Kartuli) is a complex language that is difficult to learn. It contains a complex set of rules that govern verbs, as well as many formidable clusters of consonants—for example, Tbilisi (t-BLI-si)—that can baffle and frustrate the foreign student. Other examples are *trtvili* (TR-t-vi-li), meaning "frost," and *brtskinvale* (br-ts-kin-VA-le), meaning "brilliant." Georgian also includes many glottal stops, similar to the sound that English Cockneys make when they say "bottle" (BOH-ul). Vowels are short and sharp, and the people roll their *R*s.

Fortunately all thirty-three Georgian letters correspond to only one sound each, so confusion does not arise with them. Where there are two or three syllables in a word, the stress usually falls on the first syllable. For words with four or more syllables, the situation is more complicated.

OTHER TONGUES

There are many ethnic groups in Georgia and just as many languages that are spoken as either a first or second language.

MINGRELIAN, LAZ, AND SVAN These belong to the Kartvelian group of languages. Mingrelian is spoken along the central and southern coastal areas of the Black Sea, mainly in Samegrelo. Laz is spoken mainly in parts of Georgia close to northeastern Turkey. Mingrelian and Laz were originally subdivisions of the ancient Colchian tongue.

Svan has no alphabet, and is spoken mainly at home and socially by the people of the small mountain communities of Svaneti. Svan has preserved more of old Kartvelian than Georgian, probably because of the isolation of the Svans at various times throughout history.

In the 1930s the Mingrelian and Svan people were classified collectively as Georgians, and their languages were categorized as Georgian dialects. Since then the Mingrelians and Svans have received their education in Georgian and are classified as Georgian speakers.

ABKHAZIAN There are about one hundred thousand speakers of Abkhazian in the Abkhazian Autonomous Republic, which now considers itself independent. The Georgian constitution recognizes this as the state language of Abkhazia. Abkhazian is a member of the small northwest Caucasian family of languages that includes Circassian and the almost extinct Ubykh, which is still spoken in parts of Turkey.

Abkhazian is not related to the Georgian language, and many Abkhazians speak poor Georgian, preferring instead to use Russian as their second language. The first Abkhazian alphabet was devised in 1862, but a wide selection of publications in Abkhazian became common only during the Soviet period. Television programs have been broadcast in Abkhazian since 1978.

OSSETIAN, AZERBAIJANI, AND ARMENIAN Ossetian, the language of ethnic Ossetians, is spoken in various parts of Georgia, especially in South Ossetia. It is part of the Iranian group of languages. Azerbaijani and

Armenian, the national languages of Georgia's two neighbors, are spoken by Azerbaijanis and Armenians living in Georgia.

RUSSIAN As the language of the Soviet Union and of the tsarist authorities who ruled prior to the 1917 Russian Revolution, Russian has been spoken in Georgia for two hundred years. Today it is still a popular language for those communities—such as the Ossetians, Abkhazians, Armenians, and Azerbaijanis—who do not speak Georgian well.

NAMES

As can be expected in a country with many ethnic groups, Georgians are named according to their ethnic and linguistic background. Members of Georgia's Muslim population—made up of the Azerbaijanis, Ossetians, and Abkhazians—often take traditional Islamic names, while Russians and Armenians use names from their own languages.

Popular Georgian men's names include Georgi, Nerab, Shota, David, Pavele, Alec, and Soso. Popular female names include Marina, Tamara, Lamara, Tamriko, Tsitsi, Thea, Lili, and the ubiquitous Mary.

Many Georgian surnames end in -*dze* ("son of"), or -*svili* ("child").

MEDIA

For a country with a long literary tradition, it is not surprising that Georgia has many newspapers and periodicals. Since the glasnost period of the late 1980s and subsequent independence, many new periodicals and newspapers have been published.

The Georgian constitution clearly establishes the freedom of speech and freedom of the press. In practice, however, the country falls somewhat short of that principle. In 2016, Freedom House, an organization that evaluates freedom in nations around the world, assigned Georgia the status of "Partly Free" out of a possible three levels: "Free," "Partly Free," and "Not Free." While Georgia's status is not ideal, it is better than the surrounding region, where Georgia is encircled by countries deemed "Not Free." Freedom Houses states,

"Georgia continues to have the freest and most diverse media environment in the South Caucasus, though political polarization and close links between media companies and politicians continue to negatively affect the sector." The report suggests political bias in certain privately-owned media companies, and some harassment and intimidation of journalists, saying "The level of violence and harassment aimed at journalists has been a serious problem in the past, particularly during election periods. [However,] no cases of serious violence were reported in 2015."

The state-owned, Tbilisi-based Georgian Public Broadcaster (GPB) includes Channel 1, Channel 2, and Ajaria TV, based in Batumi. There are also a number of independent commercial TV stations, and the Georgian Orthodox Church operates a satellite-based TV station called Unanimity. In 2015, a nationwide digital switchover was completed. In addition, there are several dozen private radio stations; and GPB operates two radio stations. Radio shows are broadcast in Georgian, Russian, Armenian, Azerbaijani, and English, while television programs are shown in Georgian and Russian.

About 45 percent of Georgians have access to Internet. According to Freedom House, the country's status in terms of Internet freedom, unlike its press freedom, is "Free."

INTERNET LINKS

http://ejc.net/media_landscapes/georgia
The European Journalism Centre provides a good overview of the media in Georgia.

https://freedomhouse.org/country/georgia
Freedom House reports on press and Internet freedom in Georgia.

http://www.omniglot.com/writing/georgian.htm
Omniglot gives a good introduction to and history of the Georgian language.

ARTS

The blue glass Bridge of Peace is a new pedestrian bridge spanning the Kura River in Tbilisi.

10

T HE GOLDEN AGE OF GEORGIAN arts was a long time ago. From the eleventh to the thirteenth centuries, medieval painting, poetry, literature, and architecture flourished. The time of Queen Tamar (reigned 1184—1213) was the pinnacle of this glorious age, which produced the country's great poet Shota Rustevalei, writer of Georgia's national epic poem, *The Knight in the Panther's Skin*. The Mongols invasions eventually weakened the country and brought its golden age to an end.

Georgians are naturally proud of their rich artistic heritage, but today's artists cry out for attention as well. Although there are some contemporary art galleries in Tbilisi, Georgian artists still find it challenging to find an audience. Some people blame economic difficulties for the lack of a permanent contemporary art museum in Tbilisi. Nevertheless, artists are hard at work in Georgian today, just as they were in the past.

Many Georgian artists and art lovers complain that there is no contemporary art museum in Tbilisi. There are galleries, but no permanent modern art museum, which is surprising for a national capital.

METALWORK

The Georgians were fabled in the ancient world for their skill at metallurgy. Bronze Age Georgians were highly accomplished at smelting, forging, soldering, and embossing items with a high level of precision. In the fourth and fifth centuries, Georgian jewelry was second to none in the ancient world.

Following Georgia's conversion to Christianity, monastic iconography and book illumination became important art forms. The tenth-century Ishkani Processional Cross and KhobiIcon of the Virgin Mary, and the eleventh-century Martvili Cross and silver roundel of Saint Mamai from Gelati are some of the beautiful pieces that can be seen in the Georgian State Museum in Tbilisi. The most famous piece in the museum is the tenth-century Khakhuli Triptych, which is embossed with rubies, pearls, and enamel. The Triptych is a masterpiece of medieval craftsmanship and was believed to have miraculous powers.

ARCHITECTURE

Georgians appear to have an affinity for stone, and their architecture combines the practical with the picturesque. There are many cathedrals, churches, monasteries, castles, and fortifications throughout Georgia.

The most popular style of dwelling is the rustic house known as *darbazi* (dar-BA-zi), which dates back to ancient times. The dome-type roof of the darbazi tapers into a pyramid made from wooden logs, with successive layers piling up to form a window hole at the top, which also functions as a smoke flue. Modern variations of these can be found in central Georgia, usually decorated with beautifully carved doors, lintels, and fireplaces.

The home of a Georgian nobleman, shown in this painting, features the darbazi style of architecture, with an oculus in the roof letting in light.

CHURCH ARCHITECTURE Georgian religious architecture thrived in the golden age of King David the Builder and Queen Tamar. Two designs for churches were popular: the domed type and the basilica. Domed churches have either a square or hexagonal-shaped central section. Basilica churches have a large rectangular center with aisles on each side.

Variations of the domed church first appeared in Georgia in the sixth and seventh centuries. The most famous of these is the Church of Dzhvari, which is spectacularly situated on a cliff at the confluence of the Aragvi and Kura rivers, a few miles from Tbilisi. The famous Cathedral of Svetitskhoveli ("Church of the Life-Giving Pillar") can be found at Mtskheta. It is a basilica-type church built in the eleventh century. The arcaded interior walls are covered with grotesque beasts carved in stone. The story of the building of this church is told in Constantine Gamsakhurdia's historical novel, *The Hand of the Great Master*.

The Alaverdi Cathedral in Kakheti and Bagrat Cathedral at Kutaisi also date from the eleventh century. King David the Builder founded the well-known Gelati Monastery in 1106. The monastery complex consists of three churches, an academy building, and the tomb of the king, who had also intended the monastery to be a center of learning. The development of religious architecture came to an end with the Mongol invasion in the thirteenth century.

FORTRESSES AND CAVE TOWNS Because of the many conflicts fought on Georgian soil, it is impossible to travel very far in the republic without coming across a fortress or castle. Situated on the Solalaki Ridge and dominating the skyline above the old section of Tbilisi are the ruins of the massive Narikala Fortress. Arab lords built the towers and walls in the eighth century on the site of fortifications that had been erected by King Vakhtang Gorgasali. The strategic importance of this fortress was such that King David the Builder—

The Ananuri Cathedral and Fortress is an impressive sight on the Aragvi River. The castle complex has been nominated for inclusion on the UNESCO World Heritage list.

and after him, the Mongols, Turks, and Persians—all rebuilt and extended the fortifications, making it a hybrid of styles. Part of the fortress was destroyed when gunpowder that was being stored there was struck by lightning in 1827.

Ananuri is a superb sixteenth-century fortress complex situated near the Georgian Military Highway, 40 miles (64 km) north of Tbilisi. Its crenellated walls and defensive towers make it one of the more memorable monuments along the highway. The dukes of Aragvi, a violent feudal family, built the fortress as a residence and sanctuary during their frequent feuds with rival dukes.

Georgia has some very impressive cave architecture, rivaled only by similar dwellings in the Middle East. Uplistsikhe ("the lord's fortress"), south of Gori in Kartli, is a city made of caves carved into the soft stone of the cliffs and hills that overlook the Kura River. One of Georgia's oldest urban settlements, it was built over a period of hundreds of years in the first millennium BCE. The city continued to flourish throughout antiquity, and was an important trading center in the Middle Ages, with a population of twenty thousand. It was sacked by the Mongols in the thirteenth century and never

The old cave city of Uplistsikhe, dating from the fifth century BCE, was partially destroyed by an earthquake in 2000.

regained its former importance. The weather has slowly eroded the cave city, although the shapes of the dwellings and the city walls are still visible.

The caves were used as a place of worship; an impressive church basilica dates from the ninth century. Uplistsikhe served as a prototype for the cave monasteries that developed later at David Gareja and Vardzia. David Gareja (or Garedzha) is a complex of twelve monasteries built amid the semilunar landscape of the Garedzha Hills in Kakheti, near the Azerbaijan border.

THE VARDZIA CAVES The Vardzia Caves, spectacularly situated 10,000 feet (3,048 m) above sea level in the Lesser Caucasus, form a vast complex of man-made cave dwellings, palaces, churches, and monasteries. The caves are carved out of soft tufa and were first used as secular dwellings in the fifth century BCE. A Christian religious community expanded them in the eighth and ninth centuries CE, and Queen Tamar used the caves to create a monastery and a center of Georgian culture in the late twelfth century.

The Vardzia Caves represent the apex of cave architecture and a supreme expression of the Georgian religious spirit. Some of the five hundred or so individual cave dwellings have their own small churches. The centerpiece of the complex is the Church of the Dormition, carved out of the cliff in 1184 on the instructions of Queen Tamar. The church contains many magnificent frescoes as well as inscriptions and portraits dedicated to the queen and her father, King Giorgi III. The most monumental religious fresco depicts the Virgin and Child. Other frescoes on religious themes include portrayals of the crucifixion, Jesus's descent into hell, and the raising of Lazarus from the dead.

RUSSIAN INFLUENCES Because of the tsarist Russification policy, Russia's neoclassical style imposed itself on Georgia in the nineteenth century. However, the Russians' strict notions of classical order were subverted by the flamboyant charm of the Caucasus, so a hybrid style developed. Many of these hybrid buildings can still be seen in Tbilisi.

Many large, ugly municipal buildings sprang up under the Soviet regime. The only contemporary construction that is worthy of any mention is the building of the Ministry of Highways in Tbilisi, built in 1977. Paradoxically,

Oriental styles from Georgia and other Central Asian Soviet republics influenced building styles in Soviet Russia as well.

LITERATURE

Georgia has an independent literary tradition that dates back to the fifth century CE, when a distinct Georgian alphabet came into being. The earliest works of Georgian literature were historical and religious, translating biblical and scriptural texts and describing the lives of Georgian saints. Jacob Tsurtaveli's *The Martyrdom of St. Shushanik* (476—483) is the earliest of these. The earliest Georgian chronicle, *The Conversion of Iberia*, written in the seventh century, describes the mission of Saint Nino. Georgian writing of this period was also influenced by contact with early Christian and Arabic literature, and many Persian tales were recast in Georgian form.

In Shota Rustaveli's (ca. 1172—ca. 1216) epic masterpiece, *The Knight in the Panther's Skin*, written in the late twelfth to early thirteenth centuries, Georgian medieval literature reached its zenith. Written during Queen Tamar's illustrious reign, this long epic poem embodies the cultural sophistication of the period, and reflects the influence of Chinese, Persian, and ancient Greek philosophy. It has a universal appeal and has been translated into most major languages.

After the Mongol invasions of the thirteenth and fourteenth centuries, Georgian cultural and artistic life stagnated. Georgian literature eventually revived in the sixteenth century, renewing its ties with Muslim Oriental verse. In the early part of the eighteenth century, King Vakhtang VI (1675—1737), a poet and scholar, codified Georgia's laws in the *Code of Vakhtang*, and set up Georgia's first printing press.

Following Russian annexation, Prince Alexander Chavchavadze (1787—1846) and Grigol Orbeliani (1800—1883) were the first representatives of a thriving Romantic movement among the Georgian aristocracy. In the nineteenth century many Georgian intellectuals studied in Russia and traveled throughout Europe, gaining greater exposure to new ideas. Despite heavy tsarist censorship, Georgian writers turned to social themes in the latter part of the nineteenth century, reflecting many of the political concerns that were current in Russia and Europe at the time. Two leading figures in this movement were the writers Ilya Chavchavadze (1837—1907) and Akaki Tsereteli (1840—1915). In the early twentieth century the Georgian symbolist poets experimented with new forms of poetic expression. Among these poets were Paolo Iashvili (1894—1937), Titsian Tabidze (1895—1937), and Galaktion Tabidze (1891—1959), whose movement, The Blue Horns (a reaction against realism and civic modes in Georgian literature), thrived during the years of the Georgian independence struggle, from 1918 to 1921. However, Georgian national literature was suppressed during the Soviet leader Joseph Stalin's reign, and Titsian Tabidze was executed during one of the purges of the 1930s, while Iashvili committed suicide in 1937.

Georgian literature slowly revived after the death of Stalin. Constantine Gamsakhurdia (1891—1975) was the greatest novelist of the immediate post-Stalinist period, and he introduced an unprecedented subtlety to Georgian prose. He explored Georgia's past and culture through historical novels such as *The Hand of the Great Builder* (1942) and *The Flowering of the Vine* (1955).

Otia Ioseliani (1930—2011) is a successful contemporary dramatist whose comedies *Until the Ox Cart Turns Over* and *Six Old Maids and a Man* have been staged in Germany. Chabua Amirejibi (1921—2013), a Soviet-era dissident, is noted for his narrative power on historical themes, while Otar Chiladze (1933—2009) explores Georgian myth and history through his novels. Lia Sturua (b. 1939) is Georgia's best-known contemporary woman poet.

PAINTING

Painting is a relatively recent art in Georgia, flourishing since the end of the nineteenth century. Niko Pirosmanishvili (1862—1918), popularly known as Pirosmani, was a self-taught artist who painted in a direct, primitive style. Through his depiction of everyday Georgian life at the turn of the twentieth century, he expressed the national psyche better than any other Georgian artist. He died in obscurity and his work was recognized only after his death. His paintings, such as *Woman and Children Going to Draw Water*, are displayed at the Georgian State Art Museum in Tbilisi.

Georgian painting flourished throughout the twentieth century. Mose Toidze (1871—1953) painted in the Socialist Realist style promoted by the Soviet authorities. Lado Gudiashvili (1896—1980) and David Kakabadze (1889—1952) both painted in a distinctly Georgian style, which is based on Byzantine traditions. Gudiashvili is famous for his fantastic and grotesque portrayals, especially *Fish* (1920) and *The Underprivileged* (1930). Kakabadze created skillful abstract works. Helena Ahklevediani (1901—1976) is known for her depictions of historic Tbilisi.

The painting *Six Princes (Feast)* (1905-1907) by Niko Pirosmanishvili hangs in the State Oriental Art Museum in Moscow.

MUSIC AND BALLET

Tbilisi has long had musical connections. Zakaria Paliashvili (1872—1933) is considered the father of Georgian opera. His most famous works are Abesalom and Eteri and Daisi. Tbilisi's marvelous Moorish opera house, the Paliashvili Opera and Ballet Theater, was named in his honor. His contemporary Meliton Balanchivadze (1862—1937) is also considered one of the originators of Georgian professional music. He wrote the country's first national opera, *Perfidious Daredzhan*, first staged in Tbilisi in 1926. His son, Andrei Balanchivadze (1906—1992), continued the family's musical tradition by

A man in Georgian folk dress plays the traditional string instrument called the panduri.

writing the first Georgian ballet, *Heart of the Hills*, in 1936, and a composition called *The Pages of Life* in 1961.

Dmitri Arakishvili (1873—1953) brought Georgian folk music into the mainstream, writing and composing more than five hundred pieces. He also composed a number of symphonies and choral works.

Vakhtang Chabukiani (1910—1992) is Georgia's most famous ballet dancer and choreographer. After a distinguished dancing career, he became director of the ballet troupe at the Paliashvili Opera and Ballet Theater, where he created a unique style of male stage dancing that combined the movements of both classical ballet and Georgian folk dancing.

Nina Ananiashvili (b. 1963) is artistic director of the State Ballet of Georgia (SBG). Under her leadership, the SBG is enjoying an artistic resurgence. A native of Tbilisi, Ananiashvili has won most of the major awards in ballet and has performed with almost every prestigious ballet company in the world. She has been named a People's Artist of the Georgian Republic.

FILM

Under the Soviet regime a strong Georgian movie industry developed and prospered. A former sculptor named Mikhail Chiaureli helped the Georgian branch of Soviet cinema develop during the 1920s and 1930s.

In the post-Stalin era cinema is the only artistic field where Georgian genius has reached its former heights. Like many other forms of artistic expression in Georgia, cinema became a way for people to celebrate their national spirit and culture. Many talented directors have worked in the Gruzia movie studios in Tbilisi. Giorgi Shengelaya (b. 1937) directed *Pirosmani* (1971), a movie that celebrates the life of the famous painter Niko Pirosmanichvili;

Eliso, based on a short story by Alexander Kazbegi; and *The Blue Mountains*, a satire about the Soviet bureaucracy.

The most famous movie to come out of Georgia in the perestroika (restructuring) period (1980—1991) was *Repentance*, 1984, an allegory that achieved notoriety for its grotesque depiction of the repressive era under Stalin. Directed by Tengis Abuladze (1924—1994), the movie attracted record audiences all over the Soviet Union, with seventeen million people seeing it within the first three weeks of its release. Abuladze had previously won a prize at the Cannes Film Festival in 1956 for the movie *Magdana's Donkey*. He also won the Lenin Prize for his trilogy *The Plea, The Wishing Tree*, and *Repentance*.

More recently, the movie *Tangerines*, 2013, a movie by Zara Urushadze (b. 1965), is set during the 1992—1993 war in Abkhazia. It won many awards and was nominated for an Academy Award for best foreign language film.

INTERNET LINKS

https://georgiaabout.com/tag/georgian-art
This site features the work of some of Georgia's greatest artists.

https://georgiaabout.com/2014/04/22/lado-gudiashvili
Some of the paintings of Lado Gudiashvili are displayed on this site.

http://georgiastartshere.com/georgian-history-for-newbies-georgias-medieval-golden-age
This somewhat light-hearted site takes a look at Georgia's Golden Age, a mixture of arts and history.

http://hitchhikershandbook.com/2014/05/28/david-gareja-monastery-complex-georgia
Wonderful photos of the David Gareja monastery complex are featured on this site.

LEISURE

European Square in Batumi has places to rent and park bicycles.

11

THERE IS A WELL-KNOWN GEORGIAN legend that tells of how the Georgians came to possess the country they deem the most beautiful in the world. When the world was being created, God was allotting land to the peoples of the world. The Georgians, who were too busy eating, drinking, and having a good time, showed up late. "There's no land left," God told them.

"But we were drinking a toast to your health," answered the Georgians, "Come and join us."

It is said that God enjoyed himself so much that he gave the Georgians all the land he had been saving for himself. This tale suggests much about the Georgians' high regard for their homeland.

When the Georgians are not eating, drinking, and entertaining, they enjoy the kind of leisure activities that are common throughout the world. Radio and television are popular, and people often visit some of Georgia's many museums, especially in Tbilisi, that display the country's rich cultural and artistic heritage. In summer there are many parks and nature reserves where people can walk, climb, or picnic. The most famous of these are at Pitsunda, Borzhomi, and the Forest Park of the Sukhumi Mountains.

To promote healthy lifestyles, help protect the environment, and provide improved safety for existing cyclists, the city of Tbilisi began constructing bicycle paths in 2017. Five-mile (8 km) stretches of bike lanes were added on both sides of the Mtkvari River, as well as in a couple of other city locations. After evaluating the impact of these lanes, city officials say they will decide whether to add more in the future.

Folk dancers perform outdoors in Batumi.

SONG AND DANCE

Many Georgian national characteristics emerge in traditional dancing, which is elegant, lively, and flamboyant. Dance is still a part of everyday life in the republic, and Georgians of all ages need very little excuse to begin dancing—they dance on any and every occasion. Traditional Georgian dance is chiefly masculine in form, although a few dances are exclusively for women.

The male dances are energetic, involving much high-kicking, leaping, twisting, and acrobatics. The *fundruki* (FOON-dru-ki) is a traditional dance performed by men on the tips of their toes. The *khorumi* (Ko-ru-mi), a war dance, is performed by a circle of men. The dance movements portray combat scenes; the men rear up like horses or creep as though they are hiding behind rocks.

The women's dances are less energetic, reflecting a more passive role. The women move their bodies slowly and gracefully. The *lekouri* (le-KO-u-ri) is a courtship dance performed by men and women. The dancers do not touch, but circle cautiously, flirting with each other.

Almost every village and valley has its own traditional songs and dances. Often the dances are based on a dramatic local or national occurrence from Georgia's long and eventful history. Folk song and folk dance have developed together in Georgia.

The Rustavi Choir specializes in restoring the folk music traditions of Georgia, scouring the country for half-forgotten songs that its members decipher and record before setting to music.

The republic has many professional song and dance ensembles, including the Georgian State Dancing Company, which showcases Georgian dances around the world.

MOUNTAIN SPORTS AND PASTIMES

Skiing is a popular pastime in Georgia. Situated in Kartli in the Lesser Caucasus, Bakuriani is one of the chief ski resorts and was, during the Soviet era, one of the most popular and famous downhill skiing complexes in the Soviet Union. The resort is 6,000 feet (1,830 m) above sea level and has been likened to Squaw Valley (California) in the United States for its ideal climate

A girl on a snowboard catches some air on a ski slope in Georgia.

Throughout the former Soviet Union, chess is a very popular pastime, and Georgia is no exception. The Georgians have been very successful in international competitions, and the women, in particular, have excelled in international chess. Nona Gaprindashvili (b. 1941), was the women's world chess champion for sixteen years, from 1962 to 1978. She has fought for women's equality in the chess world all her life. In 2015, at the age of seventy-four, Gaprindashi became a chess champion once again, winning the Seniors World Championship in Acqui Terme, Italy.

Another Georgian, Maya Chiburdanidze, who became the women's world champion at the age of seventeen, eventually ousted Gaprindashvili from her long reign. Chiburdanidze was women's world champion for thirteen years, from 1978 to 1991. Gaprindashvili and Chiburdanidze have the distinction of being the only two women to hold the title of grandmaster in both women's and men's chess.

Among the men, Tamaz Georgadze performed well in international and Russian chess competitions, and won the international title of Grandmaster in 1977. Since the breakup of the Soviet Union, Georgia has fielded its own chess teams at international competitions.

On a less happy note, however, the Georgian chess champion and grandmaster Gaioz Nigalidze was caught cheating at the Dubai Open Chess Tournament in 2015, bringing disgrace on himself and his country. He was subsequently banned for three years, until September 2018, and his grandmaster title was revoked. His previous tournaments were also investigated.

and conditions. Another major ski resort is at Gudauri, north of Tbilisi on the Georgian Military Highway. Built and operated as a joint Georgian-Austrian venture, Gudauri is a sparkling new complex of hotels, sports facilities, and superb downhill runs.

Climbing is also a popular sport. It attracts both locals and international climbers. Because of its high peaks, Upper Svaneti is a popular place to climb, and it has produced some of the most famous mountaineers in Georgia. One of the best-known was Mikheil Khergiani (1932—1969), who died in a climbing accident. His house in Mestia has been turned into a museum that honors his achievements. His father, Beknu Khergiani, had the distinction of being the climber who removed the Nazi flag from the top of Mount Elbrus after it had been planted there by the advancing Germans in 1943.

Another popular spot for alpinists and explorers are the slopes of Mount Kazbek, especially because of the great number of legends and myths associated with the mountain. One legend says that the Georgian Prometheus, Amirani, was chained in a cave on the mountainside as punishment for giving fire to humankind.

OTHER SPORTS

As in many parts of the world, soccer is Georgia's most popular sport. Home games are played in the capital's 78,000-capacity Boris Paichadze National Stadium, also known as the Dinamo Stadium, a soccer stadium in Tbilisi, Georgia. Kutaisi, Batumi, and Sukhumi also have well-supported soccer teams. Georgia produces many top-class soccer players, many of whom have moved abroad to play in the major European leagues centered in Germany and England. Georgia has its own rugby federation, and that sport is becoming increasingly popular.

Georgia boasts its own unique form of wrestling. Part sport and part dance, the wrestling is unusual because it is performed to music. It resembles judo in that the contestants are not permitted to use chokeholds or fight while they are lying down. Georgians have also gained wrestling honors on the world stage. Wrestling and weightlifting are by far its strongest sports at the Olympic Games. At the 2016 Summer Olympics in Rio de Janeiro, the

Tbilisi is famous for its hot sulfur baths. Rich in hydrogen sulfide, the waters have curative effects that have been appreciated by both locals and travelers through the centuries. The baths have been associated with Tbilisi throughout its history, and are said to be the reason why King Vakhtang Gorgasali moved his capital here. In the twelfth century, as many as sixty-eight different baths drew upon the plentiful underground waters.

There are many sulfur baths in Tbilisi, but the best known is the Herekle bath, situated underground and covered with a grand, domed roof. Many Georgians go to the baths to relax and subject themselves to a rigorous body massage. This massage includes being laid on a stone slab, having their bodies slapped and pummeled, being rubbed with a horsehair mitten (to remove dead skin cells), getting soaped, and finally being rinsed with a bucket of warm water.

French author Alexandre Dumas (1802–1870), in his travelogue Adventures in Caucasia, *described the experience:*

"Suddenly, when I least expected it, two attendants seized me, laid me out on a wooden bench and began to crack every single joint in my body, one after the other. Although I felt no discomfort, I was convinced they were all dislocated, and half expected that at any moment, these silent Persians would fold me up like a towel and pop me away in a cupboard. Then one of them held me still while the other positively danced up and down my whole body. He must have weighed a hundred and twenty pounds or more, but he seemed as light as a butterfly. A great sense of freedom and well-being permeated me. All my tiredness had gone and I felt strong enough to lift a mountain."

Republic of Georgia won two gold medals in weightlifting and wrestling; a silver in judo; and four bronze medals in judo, wrestling, and weightlifting.

A number of traditional folk games are still played in Georgia. Tskhenburti (ts-KEN-bur-ti), or "horse ball," is played on horseback by both men and women. It is similar to polo, which is also popular in the nation.

HEALTH RESORTS

Georgia's Black Sea coast is the location of many resort towns and beaches, and this is where many Georgians like to spend time relaxing, especially in summer. During the Soviet era government departments from all over Russia had holiday homes reserved for the use of their staff, and every summer people from all parts of the Soviet Union descended upon Georgia's beaches.

Known as Bichvinta in Georgian and Pitsunda in Russian, the republic's most famous Black Sea resort was named after the unique pine grove that is indigenous to the area. The pine grove borders a 4-mile (6.4 km) stretch of beach that is packed each summer. The sunny Abkhazian climate, the beach, the pleasant smell of pine needles, and a tenth-century church make Pitsunda one of the most popular resort towns. Because of the conflict in Abkhazia, however, it is less accessible than it used to be.

INTERNET LINKS

http://www.caucasianchallenge.com/2014/09/tbilisis-famous-baths-one-visit
This travel site offers photos and information about Tbilisi's sulfur baths.

http://georgiatoday.ge/en/news/list/101/Sports
Up-to-date news about sports can be found on this Georgia news site.

http://www.vogue.com/article/georgia-country-caucasus-travel-guide
Vogue's travel section offers "5 Reasons to Explore the Mountains of Georgia."

FESTIVALS

A young man in Georgian national dress holds his country's flag during an Independence Day celebration.

12

THE SOVIET UNION WAS OFFICIALLY atheist and religious festivals were frowned on, if not banned outright. The government created new national and secular special days to take their place. Soviet Georgia celebrated many such festivals, including Labor Day, Soviet National Day, and World War II Victory Day along with the rest of the Soviet Union.

But the popularity of the Georgian Orthodox Church never truly declined. The Georgian Church became, to some extent, a focus for Georgian nationalism during the Soviet era. It is no surprise, then, that after the demise of the Soviet Union and Georgia's subsequent independence, traditional Georgian and Orthodox festivals sharply increased in popularity. The old, Soviet-inspired days are noted on a much smaller scale or have been dispensed with altogether.

GEORGIAN ORTHODOX AND FOLK HOLIDAYS

Some folk and religious holidays are celebrated nationally, while others are particular to a town or region. In keeping with the spirit of people who enjoy feasting, a meal and festivities in the town or neighborhood square follow almost all religious services and festivals, and drinking and toasting continue late into the night.

In the major wine-producing regions of Kakheti and Imereti, it is traditional to hold festivals and celebrate the harvest while gathering the grapes in October. Balconies and windows are decorated with bunches of grapes, and songs and dancing take place when the day's work is done.

The Georgian Orthodox Church celebrates all the major feast days of the Orthodox calendar. The Georgian Church, like the Russian Orthodox Church, follows the Julian calendar, which is thirteen days behind the Gregorian calendar used by most of the world.

NEW YEAR'S

In the former Soviet states that are primarily Christian, New Year's celebrations have many of trappings that Westerners associate with Christmas. In an effort to de-emphasize Christmas, Soviet authorities moved secular Christmas festivities to New Year's and gave them new names. Therefore, Christmas trees, gifts, and a Santa-like character are now a part of New Year's celebrations. On New Year's Eve, Tovlis Papa, ("Grandfather Snow"), who wears all white clothing and has a snowy white beard, brings presents and sweets to the children.

Fireworks light up the sky in Batumi for New Year's Eve.

LOOKING A LOT LIKE CHRISTMAS

Chichilakis or Christmas trees? Saint Basil or Saint Nicholas? Father Snow or Santa Claus? New Year's or Christmas? To Western eyes, the holiday season in Georgia looks both familiar and different.

Although Western-style Christmas trees are also popular, Georgian tradition has its own type of "tree" for the holiday season. Chichilakis (shown below) are frilly white wooden ornaments made from a bough of hazelnut or walnut wood. The bough is shaved into strands of wood that remain attached to the top of the bough. The strands dry and curl into a wispy mass of white wooden frills that may then be decorated with apples and pomegranates. A chichilaki can range from a few inches tall to 10 feet (3 m) high or so.

The shaved branches are said to resemble the fluffy white beard of Saint Basil the Great, who is revered as a holiday gift-giving spirit, much like Saint Nicholas in Western Christian tradition. Father Snow, a Russian folk tale character, takes the secular form, much like Santa Claus. In the Eastern Orthodox tradition, Saint Basil's feast day is January 1, which adds yet another layer to New Year's celebrations.

On Epiphany, which falls on January 19 in the Orthodox tradition, many people burn their chichilakis—it's not unusual to have several—to symbolize the passing of the old year's troubles.

CHRISTMAS

In the Eastern Orthodox Church, with its Julian calendar, Christmas falls on January 7. With much of the merriment and magical customs being associated now with New Year's Eve and Day, Christmas is observed as a strictly religious festival. Candlelit church ceremonies are solemn and beautiful, and families gather for feasting.

Many faithful will take part in an *Alilo,* a religious procession through the streets. Leading the processions are white-robed priests carrying banners. People follow, singing carols as they walk. Some folks might dress as characters from the nativity story, while others dress in traditional Georgian attire. Some might collect money for charities along the way. Children may receive sweets.

An Alilo procession in Tbilisi on January 7 features characters from the nativity story.

EASTER

Easter is by far the most important festival on the Georgian Orthodox calendar, as it is for all Orthodox churches. Women and children prepare and dye Easter eggs, which are a symbol of renewal and rebirth. As with all Georgian festivals, family and friends gather after the church service to celebrate with a feast. Ascension Day—commemorating the ascension of Christ into heaven—is observed forty days after Easter. Candles are extinguished as part of the church ritual to symbolize Christ's physical departure from this world.

SAINTS DAYS

Saint Nino, who introduced Christianity to Georgia, is honored in May. Church services and feasts also mark the birth of Saint John the Baptist on June 24, and the remembrance of Saints Peter and Paul on June 28. The Assumption—Saint Miriam's Day (another name for the Virgin Mary)—is celebrated on August 28 in memory of the death of the Virgin Mary and the belief that she was taken up bodily into heaven.

Mtskheta's Day is observed on October 14. Mtskheta is Georgia's oldest city and the center of ancient Iberian culture. The Georgians believe that the city was named after Mtskhetos, son of Kartlos, the mythical father of the Georgian people. On Mtskheta's Day the congregation throngs in the Cathedral of Sveti-tskhoveli. This is one of the most sacred places in Georgia and is the center of the Georgian Orthodox Church. The patriarch leads a procession around the cathedral grounds, carrying banners and icons. Bells are rung to celebrate the occasion. In the town, clowns, mimes, and wrestlers entertain the people.

Saint George, the patron saint of Georgia, is honored on November 23. This is a very popular feast day because Saint George is not only a Christian symbol but also a national figure who represents the country's warlike pre-Christian past.

Many folk festivals are celebrated locally at various times of the year. On the third Sunday after Easter, for example, a special holiday in honor of Saint George is celebrated in Tbilisi and many parts of Kartli, Kakheti, Imereti, and Svaneti. Another festival is Okanoba (o-ka-NO-ba), held to mark the day Iberia adopted the Christian faith. This occurs in Gori and other parts of Kartli on the day after Easter.

OTHER RELIGIOUS FESTIVALS

Georgia's Muslim population celebrates all the major Islamic festivals, such as Eid-al-Fitr—a celebration to mark the end of the fasting month of Ramadan—and Eid-al-Adha, the Prophet Muhammad's birthday. Georgia's small Jewish community celebrates all the major Jewish festivals.

TBILISOBA

The Festival of Tbilisi, Tbilisoba (t-BLI-so-ba), occurs on a Sunday in October to commemorate the founding of Tbilisi and all things Georgian. The festival, which is the largest annual celebration in Tbilisi, is marked with a street carnival, and many of

Georgia's famous song-and-dance ensembles put on open-air performances. The celebration is not complete without the traditional personification of old Tbilisi—the roguish Kinto—clowning with a wine skin. A colorful bounty of fruits, cheeses, candy, wines, and other traditional foods are displayed by vendors.

Although the fest has an ancient autumn harvest feel to it, it's actually a new tradition, first held in 1979. The festival was suspended for a few years in the 1990s as a sign of protest and national mourning following the killing of twenty demonstrators in Tbilisi by Soviet Special Forces on April 9, 1989. The celebration resumed in 1995 and has been held annually ever since.

CIVIL HOLIDAYS

Georgians still celebrate a number of civil holidays that have survived from the Soviet era. May 1 is celebrated as Labor Day throughout the Commonwealth of Independent States, and in Georgia it is a popular spring holiday.

Georgians also observe World War II Victory Day on May 9 by laying wreaths and paying their respects to those who lost their lives in the war. During Soviet rule it was a common practice to have holidays to celebrate the achievements of certain public services, such as industry or the military. Some of these days are still observed, such as Georgian Police Day (November 22), which includes a parade of police vehicles through Tbilisi. Mother's Day has replaced the more politicized Soviet celebration of International Women's Day in March.

INDEPENDENCE DAY Georgians celebrate their independence on May 26. This day marks the country's first independence in 1918 following the 1917 Russian Revolution and the subsequent disintegration of tsarist Russia. Traditionally and historically this date is more significant to the Georgians than their break with the Soviet Union in 1991.

In recent years Independence Day has been marked by noisy displays of military strength with troops, artillery, and tanks parading down Rustaveli Avenue in Tbilisi, while warplanes fly overhead. In the early 1990s various paramilitary groups, such as the Mkhedrioni (m-ked-RIO-ni), participated in the official procession. More recently the Mkhedrioni's absence is a positive sign of the waning power of warlords and the growing strength and stability of the elected government.

INTERNET LINKS

http://agenda.ge/article/190/eng
Georgian New Year celebration traditions from ancient to current day.

http://www.georgianjournal.ge/society/32963-tbilisoba-this-weekend-georgias-most-colorful-festival.html
Gorgeous photos of the Tbilisoba festival accompany a small article about the autumn celebration.

http://www.georgianjournal.ge/discover-georgia/29255-how-georgians-celebrate-the-new-year-and-christmas.html
New Years and Christmas traditions are explained in this article.

https://www.timeanddate.com/holidays/georgia
This site lists public holidays and other special observances in Georgia by calendar year.

FOOD

An abundance of spices are displayed in a market in Batumi.

13

GEORGIAN CUISINE IS RELATIVELY unknown in the West. Outside of major cities such as New York, there are few Georgian restaurants. The cooking has a distinct flavor, with ingredients and style bearing some similarity to the cuisines of the eastern Mediterranean.

According to one Georgian creation myth, God took a break from the hard work of creating the world in order to enjoy a meal. While he was dining, he tripped over the high peaks of the Caucasus Mountains, spilling a little something from everything on his plate to the land below. That was Georgia, which became an earthly paradise, thanks to those heavenly table scraps.

Diners enjoy an outdoor meal on Vakhtang Gorgasali Square in Tbilisi.

The country's sunny climate and fertile soil have traditionally resulted in an abundance of homegrown agricultural produce. Most food is bought fresh from the market. Classic Georgian meal ingredients include lamb, chicken, fish, cheese, bread, hazelnuts, walnuts, corn, pomegranates, plums, grapes, kidney beans, eggplants, peppers, coriander, and mint. There are many regional variations.

THE GEORGIAN TABLE

Although there are many good restaurants in Georgia's towns and cities, the best place to experience the full range of Georgian cuisine is in the home. Georgians love entertaining, and they invite relatives, colleagues, friends, and even strangers into their homes at the slightest opportunity. Entertaining at the table offers Georgians the chance to express their generosity, exuberance, and sense of community. For Georgians a good meal is a well-attended table groaning under the weight of vast amounts of food and drink.

Georgian feasts typically include many dishes set out at the same time.

At home women cook and serve the food. The men do not help. Instead they sit at the head of the table toasting and entertaining guests. Georgian food is not served in conventional courses or even in any particular order. Soup may make its appearance an hour into the meal, and great platefuls of *shashlyk* (shash-LIK), or skewers of grilled lamb, and roast pork may appear late in a meal.

SUPRAS A *supra* (literally meaning tablecloth) is a traditional Georgian feast, an important part of Georgian social culture, typically hosted by a *tamada*, or toastmaster. The feast itself is a sort of banquet, with many courses laid out on the table. There are two types of supra—a festive supra called a *keipi*, and a somber supra called a *kelekhi*, which is held after funerals.

MEAT Georgia is a predominantly mountainous country where people mostly raise sheep and chicken, and this is reflected in the cuisine. *Shashlyk*,

A statue of a tamada in a Tbilisi park celebrates the importance of the Georgian toastmaster.

better known elsewhere as "shish kebab," is the most popular meat dish in the Caucasus, although chicken is also popular. *Chakhobili* (cha-ko-BI-li) is a chicken and tomato stew spiced with coriander, while *tabaka* (TA-ba-ka) is cooked by frying chicken that has been pressed between two clay plates. *Khinkali* (KIN-ka-li), or dumplings filled with ground lamb, chicken, or beef, is a local favorite. *Basturma* (BAS-tur-ma) is a thinly sliced and seasoned air-dried beef.

VEGETABLE DISHES Although the Georgian diet is heavily meat-based, vegetables accompany most meals. *Pkhala* (p-KA-la) is a vegetable puree, often made with spinach, beet, or eggplant, mixed with walnuts and vinegar,

Women sell homemade and smoked cheese at a food market in Kutaisi.

and topped with pomegranate seeds. It is generally eaten with *matsoni* (MA-tso-ni), or Georgian yogurt, and *lavashi* (LA-va-shi), a flat, flaky bread.

Lobio (LO-bi-o) consists of kidney beans baked with water and then crushed with a pestle and mixed with coriander and spices. This is often eaten as an accompaniment to meat dishes. Eggplant is also a popular ingredient. *Badrijani* (bad-RI-ja-ni) consists of baby eggplants stuffed with ground hazelnuts and herbs, served whole. *Chanakhi* (CHA-na-ki) is a mixture of eggplants, tomatoes, green peppers, and chunks of lamb cooked in a clay pot. Vine leaves stuffed with rice, herbs, and minced lamb is a popular dish throughout the Caucasus and is served with yogurt.

CHEESE AND BREAD Georgian cheese is generally made from goat's milk. There are many varieties, but *suluguni* (su-LU-gu-ni) is a typical Georgian cheese that resembles mozzarella. *Khachapuri* (kach-A-pu-ri) is a cheese pastry made by wrapping suluguni cheese in pieces of dough and baking them. This local equivalent of fast food is sold by street vendors and in cafés and restaurants. Bread is served as an accompaniment to all meals. Called *puri* (PU-ri), it is either round and crusty or long and doughlike. The latter variety is known as *dedaspuri* (de-das-PU-ri). *Lavashi* (the flat, flaky bread) is often eaten with yogurt.

A dish of tkemali sauce is garnished with dill.

SAUCES Sauces are used extensively at the Georgian table to complement, rather than mask, the primary ingredient. *Satsivi* (SA-tsi-vi), better known as the Turkish Circassian sauce, is made of ground walnuts and is generally used to accompany poached chicken. *Adzhika* (AD-zi-ka) isa hot condiment from Abkhazia made from red chilies and herbs, while *tkemali* (t-KE-ma-li) is a spicy plum sauce that is considered an essential accompaniment for shashlyk. Pomegranate chutney is also used to accompany lamb and fish dishes.

DRINKS

Georgia's varied climate means that the humid regions of Samegrelo and Ajaria are able to grow subtropical plants such as tea, while the drier central and eastern parts of the country can grow grapes for winemaking. Georgian tea is of the green variety, and is drunk at home and in teahouses. Thick, strong, Turkish coffee is also popular. Because of Turkey's historical influence in Ajaria, the best place to drink coffee is in one of Batumi's many cafés.

Georgia also produces its own brandy and mineral water. Georgian brandies are considered equal in quality to some of the more famous labels from neighboring Armenia. The best-known labels are Vardzia, Sakartvelo, Tbilisi, and Eniseli. Georgia's own mineral water, Borzhomi—from the resort of the same name—is similar to Perrier, although it is saltier and less fizzy. *Chacha* (CHA-cha), a home brewed spirit made from grape pulp, is drunk at home.

Farmers harvest grapes in a Kakheti vineyard.

WINE Georgia has a long winemaking tradition. Archaeological evidence suggests that wine was made as far back as 5000 BCE, making Georgia one of the ancient centers of viticulture. The most famous wine-growing regions are Kakheti, Imereti, Racha, and Lechkhumi. Abkhazia also produces some good wines. Although most of the wine is produced on farms, many residents of these regions have their own garden grapevines, as well as huge tubs for treading the grapes and vats for fermenting the wine. The grapes are harvested in early October.

Georgia grows more than five hundred grape varieties—a vast array for such a small country—and produces sixty different wines. Protected by the Caucasus, the republic's numerous valleys—each with its own microclimate—have ideal conditions for growing many types of grapes. The best grape varieties are Saperavi, Tsinandali, Chinuri, Mtsvane, and Tasitska. Most Georgian wines are named after the region or town in which they are produced.

During the Soviet era, Georgia produced a large part of the domestic wine consumed in the Soviet Union. In more recent years, Georgian wine producers have attempted to break into world markets, tailoring their wines to international standards.

Wine aficionados celebrate the harvest at a wine tasting festival during Tbilisoba.

INTERNET LINKS

https://georgianrecipes.net
Georgian recipes are posted with step-by-step photo instructions.

http://georgiastartshere.com/category/what/food-wine
This site features a series of articles about Georgian food and restaurants.

https://www.lonelyplanet.com/georgia/travel-tips-and-articles/flavours-of-the-caucasus-a-taste-of-georgian-cuisine
This travel site provides a good introduction to Georgian cuisine with photos.

http://www.seriouseats.com/2015/10/introduction-to-georgian-food-must-try-dishes.html
This site provides an overview of Georgian cuisine with ten top dishes and photos.

KOTMIS SATSIVI (GEORGIAN CHICKEN IN WALNUT SAUCE)

3 lbs. (1,400 g) chicken, cut into pieces
Salt, pepper, to taste
2 Tbsp butter
1 Tbsp oil
1 onion, peeled and chopped
1 cup (150 g) walnuts
4—6 garlic cloves, peeled
1 tsp coriander
½ tsp cinnamon
Large pinch of saffron or
   ½ tsp turmeric
½ cup (15 g) chopped fresh cilantro
2 Tbsp white vinegar or lemon juice
1 cup (240 mL) water or chicken stock

Season the chicken with salt and pepper.

In a large skillet, heat the butter and oil. Fry chicken over medium heat for 10 minutes, turn and cook on other side for another 10 minutes. Add onion, sauté for about 1 minute over low heat.

Add chicken stock, cover pan and continue cooking over low heat for 20—25 minutes or until chicken is done.

Meanwhile, in food processor or blender, grind walnuts, garlic, spices, and herbs together. Add chicken broth or water to thin if necessary.

When chicken is cooked, remove from pan and set aside. Add ground garlic walnut puree to pan, and stir. Simmer for about 5 minutes. Stir in vinegar or lemon juice. Return chicken to pan, turning to coat well with the sauce. Heat through and serve. Serves 4.

LOBIO (GEORGIAN RED BEAN STEW WITH WALNUTS)

This dish is traditionally served with *mchadi* (Georgian cornbread) and white cheese.

1 cup (150 g) toasted walnuts
½ cup (120 mL) olive oil
6 cloves garlic, finely chopped
1 medium carrot, finely chopped
1 large yellow onion,
finely chopped
1 Tbsp ground coriander
1 tsp hot paprika
1 lb. (450 g) dried dark red
kidney beans, soaked overnight
and drained
3 quarts (3 L) chicken stock
½ cup (15 g) finely chopped
fresh cilantro
¼ cup (7 g) finely chopped dill
¼ cup (7 g) finely chopped parsley

Place walnuts and half the oil in a food processor; puree until very smooth; set aside.

Heat the remaining oil in a 6-qt. (6 L) saucepan over medium-high heat. Add garlic, carrots, onions, chiles, and leeks; cook, stirring until golden, about 10 minutes.

Add coriander and paprika; cook until fragrant, about 1 minute.

Add beans and stock; bring to a boil. Reduce heat to medium, cook, slightly covered, until beans are very tender, 2—2 ½ hours.

Using a ladle, transfer half the beans to a blender; puree until smooth and return to pot. Stir in walnut puree, cilantro, dill, parsley, vinegar, salt, and pepper.

Serve with bread on the side.

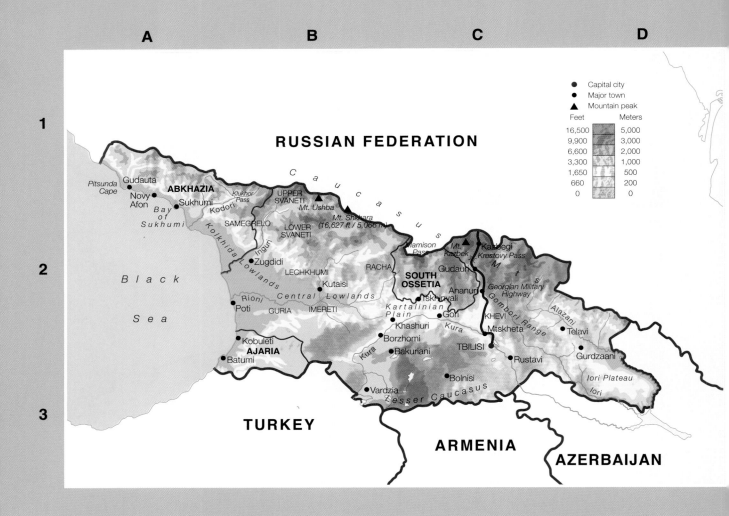

A   B   C   D

1

RUSSIAN FEDERATION

● Capital city
● Major town
▲ Mountain peak

Feet   Meters
16,500   5,000
9,900   3,000
6,600   2,000
3,300   1,000
1,650   500
660   200
0   0

Pitsunda Cape
Gudauta
ABKHAZIA
Klukhor Pass
Novy Afon
Sukhumi
Bay of Sukhumi
Kodori
SAMEGRELO
C a u c a s u s
UPPER SVANETI
Mt. Ushba ▲
▲ *Mt. Shkhara (16,627 ft / 5,066 m)*
LOWER SVANETI
Kolkhida Lowlands
Inguri
Mamison Pass
▲ *Mt. Kazbek*
Kazbegi
Krestovy Pass

2

Black Sea
Zugdidi
LECHKHUMI
RACHA
Central Lowlands
SOUTH OSSETIA
Gudauri
M t s.
Kutaisi
Tskhinvali
Ananuri
Georgian Military Highway
Alazani
Rioni
Poti
GURIA
IMERETI
Kartalinian Plain
Gori
KHEVI
Mtskheta
Gombori Range
Telavi
Khashuri
Kura
Gurdzaani
Borzhomi
Bakuriani
TBILISI
Rustavi
Kobuleti
Kura
Bolnisi
Iori Plateau
AJARIA
Batumi
Vardzia
Lesser Caucasus
Iori

3

TURKEY

ARMENIA

AZERBAIJAN

MAP OF GEORGIA

Abkhazia, A1—A2, B1—B2
Ajaria, A3, B2—B3
Alazani River, C2, D2—D3
Ananuri, C2
Armenia, B3, C3, D3
Azerbaijan, C3, D2—D3

Bakuriani, B3
Batumi, A3
Bay of Sukhumi, A2
Black Sea, A1—A3, B2—B3
Bolnisi, C3
Borzhomi, B2, C2

Caucasus Mts., B1—B2, C2
Central lowlands, B2

Georgian Military Highway, C2
Gombori Range, C2—C3
Gori, C2
Gudauri, C2

Gudauta, A1
Gurdzaani, D3
Guria, B2

Imereti, B2
Inguri River, B2
Iori Plateau, D3
Iori River, C2—C3, D3

Kartalinian Plain, B2, C2
Kazbegi, C2
Kazbek, Mt., C2
Khashuri, B2, C2
Khevi, C2
Klukhor Pass, B1
Kobuleti, B2
Kodori River, A2, B2
Kolkhida Lowlands, A2, B2
Krestvovy Pass, C2
Kura River, B2-B3, C2
Kutaisi, B2

Lechkhumi, B2
Lesser Caucasus, B3, C3
Lower Svaneti, B2

Mamison Pass, C2
Mtskheta, C2

Novy Afon, A1

Pitsunda Cape, A1
Poti, B2

Racha, B2
Rioni River, B2
Russian Federation, A1, B1—B2, C1—C2, D1—D3
Rustavi, C3

Samegrelo, A2, B2
South Ossetia, C2
Shkhara, Mt., B2
Sukhumi, A2

Tbilisi, C3
Telavi, D2
Tskhinvali, C2
Turkey, A3, B3, C3

Upper Svaneti, B1—B2
Ushba, Mt., B1—B2

Vardzia, B3

Zugdidi, B2

ECONOMIC GEORGIA

Manufacturing

- Coal
- Timber
- Wine

Agriculture

- Cattle farming
- Citrus fruits
- Corn
- Grapes
- Hazelnuts
- Potatoes
- Tea
- Tobacco
- Vegetables

Natural Resources

- Gas
- Hydropower
- Metals
- Minerals
- Oil

Services

-  Airport
- Seaports
- Tourism
- Train stations

ABOUT THE ECONOMY

GROSS DOMESTIC PRODUCT (GDP)
(official exchange rate)
$14.46 billion (2016)

INFLATION RATE
2 percent (2016)

CURRENCY
Lari (GEL)
1 US dollar = 2.42 lari (April 2017)
1 Lari (GEL) = 100 Tetri
Notes: 1, 2, 5, 10, 20, 50, and 100 lari
Coins: 1, 2, 5, 10, 20, and 50 tetri; 1, 2 lari

NATURAL RESOURCES
Forests, hydropower, nonferrous metals, manganese, iron ore, copper

AGRICULTURAL PRODUCTS
Citrus fruits, grapes, tea, hazelnuts, vegetables, livestock

INDUSTRY
steel, machine tools, electrical appliances, mining (manganese, copper, gold), chemicals, wood products, wine

MAJOR EXPORTS
vehicles, ferro-alloys, fertilizers, nuts, scrap metal, gold, copper ores

MAJOR IMPORTS
fuels, vehicles, machinery and parts, grain and other foods, pharmaceuticals

EXPORT PARTNERS
Azerbaijan 10.9 percent, Bulgaria 9.7 percent, Turkey 8.4 percent, Armenia 8.2 percent, Russia 7.4 percent, China 5.7 percent, US 4.7 percent, Uzbekistan 4.4 percent (2015)

IMPORT PARTNERS
Turkey 17.2 percent, Russia 8.1 percent, China 7.6 percent, Azerbaijan 7 percent, Ireland 5.9 percent, Ukraine 5.9 percent, Germany 5.6 percent (2015)

POPULATION BELOW POVERTY LINE
9.2 percent (2010)

WORKFORCE
2.022 million (2015)

UNEMPLOYMENT RATE
12.1 percent (2016)

CULTURAL GEORGIA

Gudauri
Helicopter skiing can be enjoyed here.

Borzhomi-Kharagauli National Park
With preservation orders dating back to tsarist times, the park is richly forested and full of wildlife.

Bakuriani
This ski/hiking resort offers magnificent views of Greater Caucasus.

Daba Monastery
This 12th-century monastery is located near a cascading 197-foot (60-m) waterfall.

Shroma Cave
Amazing stalactites and stalagmites are found in these caves.

Tbilisi
The State Museum and Treasury are located here. The museum houses a unique collection of pre-Christian gold artifacts and jewelry, and the skull of the oldest inhabitant in Europe (1.7 million years old).

Sioni Cathedral
Dating from the sixth to seventh century, the cathedral is home to the holy cross of Saint Nino, the young woman who converted Georgia to Christianity.

Tbilisi Zoo and National Parks
These are home to a great number of wildlife.

Kakheti
Visitors may tour the many Telavi wineries, castles, and monasteries here.

ABOUT THE CULTURE

OFFICIAL NAME
Georgia (Sak'art'velo in Georgian)

FLAG DESCRIPTION
A single right-angled red cross connects all the sides of a rectangular white flag. In each of the four white corners are four smaller red bolnur-katskhuri crosses. The five-cross flag appears to date back to the fourteenth century. The crosses symbolize Jesus Christ and the four evangelists. The white background is a sign of innocence, chastity, purity, and wisdom. The red color of the cross stands for courage, bravery, justice, and love.

CAPITAL
Tbilisi

POPULATION
4.9 million (2016) (3.7 million in 2014 census, not counting occupied territories and the Autonomous Republic of Abkhazia and South Ossetia)

BIRTHRATE
12.5 births per 1,000 Georgians (2016)

DEATH RATE
10.9 deaths per 1,000 Georgians (2016)

ETHNIC GROUPS
Georgian 86.8 percent, Azeri 6.3 percent, Armenian 4.5 percent, other 2.3 percent (includes Russian, Ossetian, Yazidis, Ukrainian, Kist, Greek) (2014)

RELIGIOUS GROUPS
Orthodox (official) 83.4 percent, Muslim 10.7 percent, Armenian Apostolic 2.9 percent, other 1.2 percent (includes Catholic, Jehovah's Witness, Yazidi, Protestant, Jewish), none 0.5 percent, unspecified/no answer 1.2 percent (2014)

LANGUAGES
Georgian (official) 87.6 percent, Azeri 6.2 percent, Armenian 3.9 percent, Russian 1.2 percent, other 1 percent
note: Abkhaz is the official language in Abkhazia (2014)

LITERACY RATE
99.8 percent

INFANT MORTALITY RATE
15.6 deaths/1,000 live births (2016)

LIFE EXPECTANCY AT BIRTH
total population: 76.2 years
male: 72.1 years
female: 80.6 years (2016)

TIMELINE

IN GEORGIA	IN THE WORLD
683–685 CE Khazar soldiers invades Transcaucasia.	
1089–1125 King David the Builder's reign	**1000 CE** The Chinese perfect gunpowder and begin to use it in warfare.
	1100 Rise of the Incan civilization in Peru
1172–1216 Shota Rustaveli writes epic poem.	**1206–1227** Genghis Khan unifies the Mongols and starts conquest of the world.
1184 Queen Tamar begins 24-year reign.	
1236 Mongol hordes ravish Georgia.	
	1492 Christopher Columbus sails to the Americas.
1500 Ottoman Turks and Safavid Persians both extend influence into Georgia.	
	1558–1603 Reign of Elizabeth I of England
	1789–1799 The French Revolution
1801–1804 Georgia becomes part of Russian Empire.	
	1869 The Suez Canal is opened.
	1914–1919 World War I
1918 Independent Georgian state is declared.	
1921 Soviet troops invade Georgia.	
1922 Georgian-born Joseph Stalin takes power in Soviet Union.	**1933** Adolph Hitler becomes chancellor of Germany.
1936 Armenia, Azerbaijan, Georgia, Kazakh, and Kirghiz become republics of the Soviet Union.	**1939–1945** World War II

IN GEORGIA		IN THE WORLD
	1946	
1953		NATO is founded.
Ruthless Soviet Premier Joseph Stalin dies.		
1957		
Soviets launch *Sputnik I*, first space satellite into orbit.	**1969**	US astronaut Neil Armstrong become first human on the moon.
	1986	
1990		Nuclear power disaster at Chernobyl in Ukraine
South Ossetia declares itself sovereign.		
1991	**1991**	
Georgia declares independence. Earthquake leaves 100,000 homeless.		Breakup of the Soviet Union
1994		
Abkhazia declares independence.		
1995		
Eduard Shevardnadze is elected president.		
	2001	Terrorists crash planes in New York, Washington DC, and Pennsylvania.
2003	**2003**	
President Eduard Shevardnadze resigns following Rose Revolution.		War in Iraq begins.
2004		
Mikhail Saakashvili is inaugurated president.		
2008	**2008**	
Five-day war between Russia and Georgia over South Ossetia		United States elects first African American president, Barack Obama.
2013		
Former president Mikheil Saakashvili leaves Georgia after his term ends.	**2015–2017**	ISIS launches terror attacks in Belgium, France, and England.
2016		
Georgia Dream coalition wins parliamentary elections.		
2017	**2017**	Donald Trump becomes US president.
South Ossetia holds presidential election and a referendum on joining the Russian Federation.		Britain begins Brexit process of leaving the EU.

GLOSSARY

Catholicos
Head of the Georgian Orthodox Church

chacha (CHA-cha)
Strong, home brewed spirit made from grape pulp

chakhobili (cha-ko-BI-li)
Chicken and tomato stew

cherkeska (CHER-kes-kah)
Knee-length tunic

darbazi (dar-BA-zi)
Rustic houses dating back to ancient times

Gauma … jos! (ga-u-MA … jos)
Cheers!

Golden Fleece
The fleece of the golden ram, stolen by Jason and the Argonauts from the king of Colchis

Kartvelebi (kart-VE-le-bi)
Georgians' name for themselves

khantsi (KAN-tsi)
Large goat's horn filled with wine

khinkali (KIN-ka-li)
Bell-shaped dumplings filled with ground lamb, chicken, or beef

lavashi (LA-va-shi)
Flat, flaky bread

mkhedruli (m-ked-RU-li)
Georgian script

Nartaa (NAR-ta)
Famous choir made up of elderly men

puri (PU-ri)
Bread

Sakartvelo (sa-KART-ve-lo)
Georgians' name for their country, and a term used for the United Kingdom of Georgia, first formed in CE 1008

satsivi (SA-tsi-vi)
walnut sauce

suluguni (su-LU-gu-ni)
Typical Georgian cheese

tamada (TA-ma-da)
Toastmaster

Tiflis
Old name for the capital, Tbilisi, transliterated from Russian.

Transcaucasia
Collective name for the countries of the Caucasus: Georgia, Armenia, and Azerbaijan. Transcaucasia was a republic within the Soviet Union from 1922 to 1936.

FOR FURTHER INFORMATION

BOOKS

Goldstein, Darra. *The Georgian Feast: The Vibrant Culture and Savory Food of the Republic of Georgia.* University of California Press, 1993, updated ed. 2013.

Goltz, Thomas. *Georgia Diary: A Chronicle of War and Political Chaos in the Post-Soviet Caucasus* 2nd Edition. New York: Routledge, 2015.

Jones, Alex, and *John Noble, Tom Masters, Virginia Maxwell:* Lonely Planet. *Georgia, Armenia & Azerbaijan. 2016.*

de Waal, Thomas. *The Caucasus: An Introduction*. New York: Oxford University Press. 2010.

WEBSITES

BBC News. Georgia Profile—Timeline. http://www.bbc.com/news/world-europe-17303471

CIA World Factbook. Georgia. https://www.cia.gov/library/publications/the-world-factbook/geos/gg.html

Eurasianet.org. Georgia. http://www.eurasianet.org/resource/georgia

Georgia About. https://georgiaabout.com

Georgia Today. http://georgiatoday.ge

Georgian Journal. http://www.georgianjournal.ge

Government of Georgia. http://gov.ge/index.php?lang_id=ENG

MUSIC AND FILM

Alilo: Ancient Georgian Chorales. Rustavi Folk Choir. Unlimited Media, 2011.

Sacred Georgian Chants, Georgia Harmony Choir. Jade Records, 2008.

Tangerines. Zara Urushadze. First Run Features, DVD release, 2015.

BIBLIOGRAPHY

Antelava, Natalia. "Georgia purges education system." BBC News, July 29, 2005. http://news.bbc.co.uk/2/hi/europe/4724213.stm

Bardzimasvili, Temo. "Georgia Kicks Off New Year with Post-Modern Christmas Tree." Eurasianet. December 22, 2009. http://www.eurasianet.org/departments/insight/articles/eav122309.shtml

BBC News. Georgia Profile—Timeline. http://www.bbc.com/news/world-europe-17303471

CIA World Factbook. Georgia. https://www.cia.gov/library/publications/the-world-factbook/geos/gg.html

Corso, Molly. "Georgia's Elderly Remarkable, But Record-breaking?" Eurasianet, April 15, 2010. http://www.eurasianet.org/departments/insightb/articles/eav041610a.shtml

Ellena, Monica. "Georgia: Healthcare Costs Making Health Ministry Wheeze." Eurasianet, October 7, 2015. http://www.eurasianet.org/node/75446

Freedom House. Georgia. https://freedomhouse.org/country/georgia

Georgia About. https://georgiaabout.com

Georgian Journal. "Georgia No. 1 among the countries that have deadliest air pollution." *Georgian Journal*, June 28, 2016. http://www.georgianjournal.ge/society/32635-georgia-no-1-among-the-countries-that-have-deadliest-air-pollution.html

Gerontology Research Group. Table B, Verified Supercentenarians (as of January 1, 2015). http://www.grg.org/Adams/b.HTM

Hug, Adam. "Traditional religion and political power: Examining the role of the church in Georgia, Armenia, Ukraine and Moldova." The Foreign Policy Centre, October 2015. http://fpc.org.uk/publications/orthodox

Jewish Discoveries and Harry D. Wall. "WATCH: Forget Atlanta—This Is the Georgia on My Mind." *Haaretz*, February 7, 2015. http://www.haaretz.com/israel-news/videos/1.640351

Kucera, Joshua. "Where Europe Begins, or Where It Ends?" Slate, January 30, 2017. http://www.slate.com/articles/news_and_politics/roads/2017/01/georgia_insists_that_it_s_a_european_country_what_does_that_really_mean.html

Lomadze, Maka. "How Georgians Celebrate the New Year and Christmas." *Georgian Journal*. January 9, 2015. http://www.georgianjournal.ge/discover-georgia/29255-how-georgians-celebrate-the-new-year-and-christmas.html

Morison, Thea. "NDI Polls: Georgians View Russia as Biggest Threat to their Country." *Georgia Today*, May 15, 2017. http://georgiatoday.ge/news/6558/NDI-Polls%3A-Georgians-View-Russia-as-Biggest-Threat-to-their-Country

NDI. "NDI Poll: Georgians Increasingly Support EU And Euro-Atlantic Aspirations; View Russia as a Threat." May 12, 2017. https://www.ndi.org/publications/ndi-poll-georgians-increasingly-support-eu-and-euro-atlantic-aspirations-view-russia

INDEX

INDEX